The CHALLENGE

of AFRICA

K. A. Busia

FREDERICK A. PRAEGER, *Publisher*
New York

BOOKS THAT MATTER

First published in the United States of America in 1962 by
Frederick A. Praeger, Inc., Publisher
64 University Place, New York 3, N. Y.

© 1962 by Frederick A. Praeger, Inc.

Library of Congress Catalog Card Number: 62-21607

Manufactured in the United States of America

To My Wife

Contents

Preface   3

Part I: *THE CHALLENGE OF CULTURE*

1. Introduction   7
2. Treatment of the Sick and Funeral Rites in
   Akan Culture   11
3. Akan Values and the Wider Context of
   African Cultures   33

Part II: *THE CHALLENGE OF COLONIAL EXPERIENCE*

4. The Invasion of Technology   51
5. The Impact of European Government and
   Administration   65
6. The Challenge of Education   79

Part III: *THE CHALLENGE OF COMMON HUMANITY
AND MORALITY*

7. This Dark Skin   97
8. The Challenge of Morality   107

Part IV: *THE CHALLENGE OF RESPONSIBLE
EMANCIPATION*

9. Whither Development?   117
10. African Cultures and the Challenge of
    Industrialization   129
11. The Challenge of Nationalism   139

The CHALLENGE of AFRICA

Preface

THE African continent has always presented challenges. When the Roman historian Pliny remarked that "Africa always offers something new," he must have been thinking of the new products coming out of Africa—corn, gold, slaves. What other unknown products did that strange continent hold?

For centuries, the unknown interior of Africa challenged penetration, and little was known of that large continent covering 11.6 million square miles. The vast Sahara to the north, the impenetrable forests in the center, the great rivers (the Congo, the Nile, the Niger, the Zambezi), the miles of smooth unbroken coastline—all these defied the most intrepid explorers. And so did the little mosquito and the inhospitable climate.

Comparatively little is known of the history of the great continent, where, as deduced from recent archaeological discoveries, the world's earliest man lived some 700,000 years ago. Africa challenges by what is known of it, as well as by what is unknown. Its estimated population of 280 million is composed of five races—Bushmanoid, Caucasoid, Negroid, Mongoloid, and Pygmoid—of various shades of pigmentation. They are not all black, and they speak more than 800 different languages.

Today, it is African nationalism that challenges. The demands for justice, emancipation from colonial rule, and freedom and dignity for the individual, the aspirations for the high standards of living that contemporary science and technology have made possible, and the search for self-confidence and self-respect based on a past rediscovered and reappraised—all these are challenges posed by Africa to herself no less than to the rest of mankind.

Dealing with four major aspects—the challenge of culture, the challenge of colonial experience, the challenge of common humanity and morality, and the challenge of responsible emancipation—I have undertaken to examine the meaning and implications of the challenges posed by contemporary Africa both in the light of the situation in Africa and in the context of international relations and world peace.

I have dispensed with the list of those to whom I should express thanks and acknowledgments because it would be so long, despite the brevity of my book. Faithful to the traditions of the culture in which I was brought up, I acknowledge with gratitude my sense of dependence on many, living and dead, from whom I have learned and who in various ways have helped me with this work.

K. A. B.

July, 1962

I

THE CHALLENGE OF CULTURE

1. Introduction

WHEN African nationalists demand self-government, ask for technical aid, or seek loans for development projects, they seem to belong unquestionably to the twentieth century; but when they talk of African culture or African personality, they seem to be harking back ominously to an anachronistic, primeval Africa.

Yet this quest for Africa's own culture, for something that is the unique creation of Africa's own peoples, is as much an aspect of contemporary African nationalism as are parliamentary institutions or development plans. It is one of the signs of Africa's emancipation. Physical enslavement is tragic enough; but the mental and spiritual bondage that makes people despise their own culture is much worse, for it makes them lose their self-respect and, with it, faith in themselves.

Nevertheless, there is apt to be more emotion than rationality, more fantasy than objectivity in much that is portrayed as African culture.

Africa is a vast continent, inhabited by communities that

have had different historical experiences. One should be chary in describing as African culture the traditions and way of life of any one community. But we often understand the greater from the smaller—moving legitimately and logically from the particular to the general—and the experience of one African community may help us to understand, by comparison or contrast, the problems of the larger whole.

Seeking a better understanding of the problems of African culture in the context of present-day changes, I should like to begin by discussing certain aspects of the culture of the Akan peoples, who constitute more than half the population of Ghana. (There are also Akan communities, as a linguistic subgroup, in Liberia, Ivory Coast, Togo, Dahomey, and Nigeria.)

In 1947, when I was in the Administrative Service of the Government of the Gold Coast (now Ghana), I was asked to undertake a social survey of the coastal town of Sekondi-Takoradi. I found the growth of numerous associations to be one of the most striking features of the development of town life. These associations catered to various interests—social, religious, economic, and political; but whatever their primary objectives, they offered members the prized benefit of fellowship and consolation in bereavement, or of a well-attended burial at death. The interest in funeral rites was so widespread that it seemed to me to be a subject calling for special study. Accordingly, I began such a study.

The works of historians and anthropologists provide evidence that everywhere there are rituals connected with the dead, and that these rituals are invariably based on the assumption that there is a life beyond death. There is a general belief that death is not an end, but a beginning. Yet, as my study of the funeral rites of the Akan peoples progressed, I found that I was learning more about their ideals and values in *this* life than about life hereafter. The study of rituals and beliefs connected with the dead became rewarding as a means of understanding their conceptions of life and their interpretation of the universe around them. I found that I was getting at the heart of Akan thought and life, at the basis of Akan culture.

2. *Treatment of the Sick and Funeral Rites in Akan Culture*

THE solemn beats of the talking drums rend the silence of the evening. A death is announced. The chief has lost a kinsman. The skillful Akan drummer, erudite in traditional history and usages, conveys condolences to the ruler:

Condolences, condolences, condolences!
Noble ruler, we share your grief.
We sympathize with you in your bereavement.
We have, since we arose from ancient times,
Been exposed to incessant suffering.
The ogyapam tree and its ants are from antiquity,
The Creator created Death, and Death killed him.
Thou deceased, condolences, condolences, condolences! *

The drummer's condolences are conveyed in epigrams, each of which poses a riddle. Akan drum language is full of riddles that conceal reflective thought and philosophy. The cryptic message is pregnant with meaning. It conveys two consolatory ideas about death.

The Akan word that the drummer uses for the Creator,

---

* Translated by J. H. Nketia, *Funeral Dirges of the Akan People* (London: Townsend, 1956), p. 125.

11

Odomankoma, signifies one who is infinite, eternal, having no beginning and no end. Yet the drummer says on the drum, "The Creator [the Infinite, the Eternal] created Death, and Death killed him." What is one to make of this? Can Death kill the Eternal One? The older members of the drummer's audience, those who are well versed in Akan lore, will understand the message. Indeed, some of them will attend the funeral wearing the *adinkra* cloth of mourning, bearing the traditional design *Nyame bewu na mawu* (As long as God is not dead, I shall not die, or, more positively, As long as God lives, I shall live). The drummer is saying in effect: Condolences, noble ruler, condolences; as long as God is not dead, death is not an end, but a new beginning. It is the drummer's way of conveying the universal belief that there is a life beyond death. That is why the message ends with an address to the deceased. He, too, is offered condolences, for he is able to hear it in the other life just begun.

There is another pregnant epigram in the drummer's message:

> We have, since we arose from ancient times,
> Been exposed to incessant suffering.
> The ogyapam tree and its ants are from antiquity.

The ants not only harass the ogyapam tree, they kill it; yet the ants and the tree were created together from the beginning; that is to say, the tree was destined to die; it is the law of the Creator. "The Creator created Death, and Death killed him." The drummer is emphasizing the inevitability of death. Man must die. The drummer is saying to the ruler: Condolences; do not mourn; remember the Creator made man to die; and when the destined time comes, it is not only beyond the skill of the physician to save the sick, but also beyond the Creator himself to exercise his power to save this man, for the Creator has decreed that every man must die, and so he is unable to stop Death from exacting the payment due him.

This is Akan thought about death. It is more directly expressed in a funeral song:

> Where does one go and never return?
> It is the World of the Departed.
> Everybody is a debtor to Death.*

Every man must pay the debt; no one can be exempted. Nevertheless, everywhere, man tries by whatever knowledge and skill he possesses to stave off Death, never yielding until Death, too strong for mortal skill, exacts the payment of the debt due him.

We begin our study of Akan funeral rites by observing the treatment of the sick. At the bedside of the Akan who is fighting man's ceaseless battle with Death, we shall learn much that is germane to our study of culture.

In traditional Akan society, most adults were expected to know what readily available herbs might be used for certain common ailments. If anyone felt ill, he would try one or another of these remedies. If this failed, his near kinsmen would call in a "traditional healer."

Among the Akan, three types of healers treated diseases. The "general practitioner" (*adunsifo, sumankwafo,* or *asumanfo*) had knowledge of many plants, their roots and leaves, and the diseases they might be expected to cure. The second type of healer also had expert knowledge of herbs, but in addition, he possessed powerful charms or the secret of divination, or he knew how to deal with witchcraft (*abirifo, bonsam komfo*). Through the third type of healer, the priest, a god might be consulted at his shrine about the nature, the cause, and the cure of an illness.

* Ibid., p. 124.

The first task of the traditional healer was to "diagnose" the illness—that is, to find out its nature and cause, and whether or not it would end in the death of the patient. The search was for psychological or supernatural causes. It was believed that some diseases were caused by a man's own evil acts, some by supernatural agencies (witchcraft, for example), and some by the gods or ancestors.

Causes were assigned after questioning a patient, after consulting a god at his shrine, or after divination. Using one method of divination, the healer would break an egg and read the portents from the position of its parts; depending upon whether the broken halves faced up or down, and whether they were even or uneven, he would divine whether the illness would be fatal or not, whether the patient should consult another, more powerful healer. Some healers divined by sprinkling a powdered mixture on the patient; others by gazing into water. It is significant that the word used when a patient consulted a priest was *abisa,* putting a question, eeking an explanation.

If the healer decided to try to treat the patient, the sick m n's kinsfolk appointed one from among themselves and int oduced him to the healer as the patient's *Okyigyinafo,* his s pporter, or literally, the one who would "stand behind" him. This representative of the kinsfolk would discuss with the h ler all matters concerning the treatment of the patient. He would be responsible for any fees to be paid and for procuring any supplies the healer required.

The appointment of such a representative was enjoined by custom. Everyone looked to his kinsfolk for support and security; their failure to name an *Okyigyinafo* would amount to disowning the patient. No Akan family would fail a relative in this way, for it would be a standing reproach to the family.

The kinsfolk would select, in addition to the representative, one or more persons to nurse and attend the patient.

If the man was married, his wife (or wives) would nurse him. If the illness was serious or protracted, there would be a blood relative attending him as well.

Before he prescribed any medicines for the patient, the healer would discuss with the family representative the deposit *(ntoase)* that should be paid. The deposit normally consisted of a small sum of money, sixpence or a shilling, plus a fowl and either a whole bottle or a half bottle of rum. Every healer had his attendants *(sunkwafo)*, who ran errands for him, collected herbs and roots as he directed, or accompanied him when he collected these remedies himself. The attendants usually received a portion of the deposit, so that they would "go with speed to the woods to fetch the medicines with which their master would cure the patient." If the patient got better, they also received a portion of the fee that was subsequently paid.

The art of healing was inseparable from religious belief and practices. The healer would use the rum provided as part of the deposit to pour a libation to the gods. "Power is in the hands of God." Thus the healer poured libations to God, the Supreme Being, to Mother Earth, to his ancestors, his gods, and his charms and amulets; he asked them all to help him, so that whatever root or herb he plucked for the patient, whatever he gave him to drink, might be efficacious in restoring him to health. Thus the healer began by seeking supernatural aid, for he believed that without this he could not cure the patient. At the end of the prayer, he sent his attendants, or went himself, to collect the leaves, the roots, and the pieces of bark that he would give the patient. In the woods, if he needed the bark of a tree such as the "mighty" odum tree (iroko), he would offer a prayer. Pouring a libation, he would say, "O God, the Dependable One, here is drink. O Earth, here is drink. Mighty odum tree, here is drink. It is for no evil cause that I call on you; it is —— who is ill, and I have come to scrape off a piece

of your bark to make medicine for this patient. Stand behind
me that he may be restored. Here is drink; here is drink;
here is drink." Only then would the healer cut the bark.

When the healer and his attendants returned from the
woods, he would place before the patient all the remedies
that had been collected. He would require more things—
new cooking pots, for example, or calabashes, pepper, durra,
sometimes the parts of rare birds or of animals—which the
family representative would have to find. The more serious
the illness, the more medicines would be prescribed. The
healer might even require that a separate hut be erected for
the patient.

The family representative and the family attendants were
given detailed instructions about the use of the various
medicines and about taboos and observances. There might
be medicine for the patient to drink, to use in his bath,
to rub on his skin, to take in his food, to apply to his
anus; medicine for syringing, medicine to place in incisions
made on the body. Various procedures and rules had to be
observed. The attendants were told that when one medicine
was being boiled, the pot should be covered with plantain
leaves and only a small hole left for pouring out the medicine; in another case, the pot in which the medicine was
boiled was to stand on a pad of leaves and never to touch
the ground. When incisions were made on the joints of the
patient, the attendants were to have him stand on a broom.
The attendant who fetched water from the river for boiling
the medicines was forbidden to talk to anyone on his way
to or from the river. Sometimes the attendants were to add
pepper or durra or lime to certain medicines. Often during
the course of the treatment, the patient was to be denied
certain foods—palm oil, groundnut, yams, chicken, eggs,
salt, onions, okras, pepper, or meat, according to the disease.
The patient was not allowed to talk at certain times; at

others, he was advised not to nurse anger or hatred against anyone.

When food taboos were prescribed, those who tended the patient also observed them, for by eating what was forbidden to the patient they might defile the medicines and so destroy their potency. The magical aspects of the treatment were emphasized by the fact that the patient's attendants were often required to be girls who were virgins or boys who had not reached puberty. If the patient was a minor, his mother would observe the taboo on his behalf.

The healer's fee was sometimes settled after the commencement of the treatment. More often, the patient himself, or his family, promised in advance what they would give if the patient got better. When the patient felt fully recovered, he informed the healer that he felt completely restored to health and asked for the rite of purification to be performed.

Recovery from serious illness was marked by a rite of purification—to wash away any uncleanness that may have caused the illness. The day fixed for the rite was usually the patient's natal day—i.e., the day of the week on which he was born *(kra-da)*. Every Akan has a first name corresponding to the day of the week on which he was born, the day on which he "purifies his soul." On the morning of that day, the patient would take his bath early and would wear a white cloth. Members of his family would join him and would wait with him in his house for the healer and the healer's attendants.

After everyone had arrived, and after the customary courtesies of greeting and hand shaking, the healer would ask for his fee or for the votive offering *(aboade)* promised him. Like the deposit, this usually consisted of money, rum, and a fowl (or sometimes a sheep). When it had been handed over, fresh water was fetched from the river, in a new calabash

that had never been used previously. Some sand from the
river was put in the water, together with three eggs and
three leaves of the *adwere* plant, used in religious cere-
monies. The healer, his attendants standing behind him,
then poured a libation to the gods and ancestors, and
thanked them for helping him to bring health to the patient.
Followed by those who had tended him during his illness,
the patient stepped forward. He moved his cloth down to
his waist and stood before the healer, who took an *adwere*
leaf out of the water and, with it, sprinkled water three times
over the patient, saying, "Cleansing to you, cleansing,
cleansing; if anything I forbade you to eat should touch
your lips, may it not harm you; blessing and long life
to you." Then the patient and, after him, his kinsmen
thanked the healer and his attendants and shook hands with
them. While the others drank, the patient completed the
rite of purification. Going to the calabash of water and
sitting beside it, he scooped some of the water into his
mouth with both hands and spat it out. He repeated this
three times. Then he took one of the leaves of the *adwere*
plant, and with it, he sprinkled himself three times with
water. Then he took one of the eggs, and having circled it
three times around his head, to symbolize the taking away
of all uncleanness and evil from him, he broke it on the
ground. If the halves faced upward, it was a sign that his
soul had accepted the sacrifice. His kinsmen would give him
gifts of money, eggs, fowl, and other food, some of which
was cooked and sent to friends and relatives to inform them
of his recovery and sanctification. That day the patient kept
as a sacred day and refrained from doing any kind of work.

The main object here is not so much to give a detailed
account of the methods of curing disease as to illustrate
the procedure and the ideas behind it. A disease was the
concern of a man's family, which took responsibility and
supported him throughout his illness. The healer who

cured diseases relied more on the magical properties of the herbs and roots he used than on their chemically remedial properties. "It is spirit acting on spirit, not antitoxin on toxin."* It would be more accurate to say "power acting against power," for although Akan religion is characterized by animism, not all nature is believed to be animated. But all nature is charged with power, in varying degrees of potency. Both patient and healer believed that an illness had psychological or supernatural causes and that its cure depended on the aid of spiritual and superhuman powers. They believed also that spiritual uncleanness was an element of ill-health and that the cleansing of the soul was necessary for health. When, for example, a patient was made to stand on a broom while being treated, it was to symbolize this cleansing. The broom sweeps filth away from the home to keep it healthy; so the soul must be swept of filth to keep the body healthy. We shall discover the elaboration of these ideas in the rituals that pertain to the dead.

In spite of all the efforts of traditional healers, the patient might die. "The Creator created Death." To the Akan, death is a return to the World of Spirits *(Asaman)*. "Whenever a child is born in this world," according to Ashanti belief, "a ghost-mother mourns the loss of her child in the spirit world."† And whenever there is a death in this world, there is a welcome in the spirit world.

It was believed that everyone was a "debtor to Death"; nevertheless, every death had to be explained, for the fact that every man had to die did not explain why a particular person died at a particular time and place or in a particular manner.

A traditional healer called in to aid the sick attempted to discover the psychological or supernatural causes of the

* R. S. Rattray, *Religion and Art in Ashanti* (London: Oxford University Press, 1927), p. 148.
† Ibid., p. 59.

illness. This seemed to be the prime object of his "diagnosis." In the same way, when death occurred, the explanation that satisfied, and the one that was sought, was not a scientific explanation of the nature of the disease that killed the patient. Not that diseases were unknown, or that the causal relationship between sickness and death was not appreciated. A wide range of illnesses was known, and most traditional healers knew the particular herbs or other remedies to apply for at least some of the known ailments. Among these were malaria, piles, scrofula, goiter, headache, various stomach complaints, rheumatism, Guinea worm, toothache, measles, chicken pox, smallpox, leprosy, paralysis, sleeping sickness, gonorrhea, dysentery, ringworm, different kinds of boils, and so on.

It was also recognized that deaths resulted from accidents. It was not uncommon for a man to die after being bitten by a snake while he was working on his farm, for a tree to fall and kill someone during a storm, for a wall to collapse, for a man to stumble and fall dead on the ground, or for a man to die from gunshot wounds or drowning or burns. These were recognized as immediate causes, but they did not satisfactorily explain death. Why, for example, did a well-known hunter, who knew the familiar sounds and smells of the wood, why did he, clear-sighted, sober, and in broad daylight, shoot at what he saw to be a beast, but what turned out to be a man? He was sure it was a beast before he fired his gun. But after, a man screamed, fell, and died, and on going to him, the hunter recognized a neighbor, a kinsman. Why did it happen so? Why did a disease that had on many occasions responded to the traditional healer's treatment fail to respond in a particular case? Many others had had the same disease and had been successfully treated with the same remedies. Why did this particular patient die when the others had recovered?

The Akan did not look to natural philosophy or for physical answers to these questions. They were outside natural philosophy. Some deaths were believed to be caused by persistent immoral conduct. If a person known to be iniquitous died in his youth, it was said that he had died prematurely because of his wickedness. His death was attributed to that vice to which he was known to be particularly prone. Men died from drunkenness, for example, from licentiousness, from the practice of thievery (in particular, the stealing of produce from other people's farms), or they died because they showed disrespect for their elders. Offenses committed by a person against blood relatives were believed to cause many deaths. Insulting or disrespectful conduct toward one's elders was such an offense; breaking incest taboos, adultery with one's uncle's or brother's wife, failure to discharge the obligations due to blood relatives, beating one's mother, father, uncle, elder brother, or one of their wives, failing to care properly for the wives or children of a dead relation, and dissipating inherited property were other such offenses. If a person known to be guilty of any of these things died, adequate explanation was offered by his misconduct. Either it was said that his ancestors had punished him with death because of his bad conduct, or it was said that his own soul had killed him because it felt disgraced by his conduct.

Ancestors and dead relations were believed to punish their living descendants for sins both of commission and omission. The ancestors were the guardians of the society's morality, and they chastised those who failed in their duty. The explanation often heard was: "He told lies about the property, and the ancestors killed him," or "His uncle's ghost killed him because he failed to look after his children," or "His ancestors felt disgraced by his conduct, so they killed him."

Just as bad conduct caused premature death, old age bore witness to good conduct. When a very old man or woman died, the body, after it had been bathed, was marked with white clay, three lines on the forehead, three on the ear, three on the chest, three on each shoulder, and three on the neck. This was to signify that the deceased had lived virtuously and had been granted long life as a result.

The gods were also believed to punish transgressors with illness or death. Like the ancestors, the gods killed those who disobeyed their laws or committed offenses proscribed by custom, and they killed those against whom a curse was invoked. Many deaths were ascribed to curses. "If the one who stole my cloth does not return it, when he drinks of this river, may he die." "Whoever stole from my farm, if he does not confess, may the god —— kill him." These were common imprecations, and often the priest of a god, on being consulted about a patient, would declare that the patient would die because he stole or told lies and had been put under a curse. If the patient did die, his death was deemed to have been sufficiently explained.

It was also believed that a man could die from a curse invoked by himself. "If I am not speaking the truth, may I die if I drink of the river Tano," "May the ancestors take me away," "May the god —— kill me"—all were common imprecations. If shortly after making such an utterance, the man fell ill and subsequently died, the cause of his death seemed obvious.

Besides invoking the gods and ancestors, certain craftsmen could call upon the tools of their trade in a curse against anyone who stole their handiwork. A blacksmith could invoke his anvil or his hammer; a weaver, his loom; a potter, his potter's clay or one of his pots. A blacksmith would say, "If the one who stole my hoe does not return it, may this hammer kill him." A potter could utter a similar imprecation and smash a pot on the ground. If, after this, anyone who might be suspected died, it was said that the anvil, or hammer or loom or pot, had caused his death.

But it was to witchcraft that most deaths were ascribed. Even deaths from accidents—from falling trees, from snake bites—were attributed to witches. In the example already cited of a hunter who shot a man he mistook for an animal, it was said that it was because the hunter was bewitched that he mistook a man for a beast and shot him. If a priest of a god had been consulted, he might have said that the hunter's uncle, grandmother, grandfather, even his mother or father, caused him to kill the man. The priest might have explained that the relative was aggrieved because the hunter had not given him any of the game he had previously killed.

If a well-to-do or successful person died, it would be said that some blood relative had killed him by witchcraft. Among the Akan, the witch was believed to be within the extended family lineage. If a person possessed the power of witchcraft, he used it to "eat" within his own lineage— that is, he used it against his blood relatives.

While a man lay ill, there would be various speculations about and various efforts to discover the supernatural causes of his illness. There was eagerness, too, to find out whether or not he would recover. Certain events were regarded as foreboding death. Omens were often conveyed through the dreams of close relations. When a close relative of the patient reported that he had dreamed that it was raining, or that there was a meeting of all the members of the lineage, or that he saw members of the lineage who had been dead, his dream was taken as a sign that there would be a death within the lineage. If any of the pots the traditional healer had filled with herbs for the patient broke while still in use, it portended the patient's death. Other portents of death were the singing of the bluebird at night within hearing of the patient's room, or the appearance of a row of black ants near the patient's room or near any of the pots containing his medicines. If someone who was sent to col-lect roots and herbs to be used by the patient saw a snake

burial, when it was dropped in the grave. Careful attention was paid to these details of ritual. They protected the living against the malignant powers of the newly dead.

When the body had been bathed, it was taken to another room and dressed. A bed was prepared, and the body was put on it, lying, among the Akan, on its left side, and facing eastward. Hence one of the euphemistic ways of saying a person is dead is to say "he has lain on his left."

The relatives then sent runners to inform the chief of the town and other interested persons of the death. If someone died between forenoon and sundown, the relatives usually kept it quiet till after sundown, when people had already eaten. Custom enjoined fasting, but if the death was announced after sundown, this fasting could begin the following day, at the same time as the funeral.

After the relatives and the chief had been informed, news of the death was made public. The close kinsmen and kinswomen in the house, who till then had controlled their feelings, burst into wailing. If the status of the deceased warranted it, guns were fired, and the drummer joined the chorus by beating a message of condolences on his drums. Neighbors rushed into the house and joined in the lamentations, the women singing dirges as they wailed. These dirges expressed the singers' emotions, extolled the dead, or philosophized on human life and death. One such dirge said:

> This is for me a sad and memorable day;
> Be quick and let us depart;
> No place here [on earth] is safe;
> No one reigns forever on the throne of Time.

There was drumming between this period and the burial, and music was performed by bands of musicians. Dancing was not inappropriate. In bodily movements and meaningful gestures, the dancer spoke of sorrow, of bereavement, of struggle, or rest; or he conveyed his condolences, or simply danced away his grief, for sorrow and mirth could be expressed in the same rhythms.

Music, with its rich and varied beat, provided an outlet for the emotions. It afforded an opportunity for expressing sympathy to the bereaved and for sharing the joy of sound and rhythm. It expressed solidarity in an emotion that was shared by all.

Death is a separation, and to those who are closest to the deceased, it is a painful one. The sense of loss was given expression in three of the four phases of Akan funeral rites. The frantic outburst of wailing that publicly announced the death, and drew neighbors to the scene, was the first such expression. When the neighbors arrived, they joined in the wailing, and a stunning din of lamentations filled the air.

The dead was given a last feast. Women were selected from both the paternal and the maternal relatives to cook food. This food, which consisted of a wide variety of dishes, including those of which the deceased was particularly fond, was then set before the corpse. The maternal kinsmen provided the chicken, the meat, and the other foodstuffs required for the preparation of the dishes. Sometimes sheep were procured. Children attending the funeral could be given some of the food prepared for the deceased, but adults were expected to fast.

All the blood relatives, including the children and grandchildren of the deceased, shaved their hair, which was then heaped at the entrance to the house. A large quantity of hair indicated to observers that the deceased had many relatives to mourn him. It was deemed a great honor to leave behind a large number of children and grandchildren to participate in one's funeral rites.

The grandchildren, after shaving their hair, smeared themselves with clay and went up and down the streets, singing:

Condolences, condolences, condolences!
Grandpa [or Grandma] is dead; hearken!
Grandpa [or Grandma] is dead; hearken!
Let no one wail.

It was a song of triumph to the deceased. It was a great
honor for him to have lived to a good old age and to have
left behind a large number of grandchildren. He was judged
to have been victorious in life, and his body was smeared
with clay—a mark of victory. Hence the grandchildren's
request, "Let no one wail."

Despite the request that no one mourn, when the grandchildren returned from the street to the house, all present
surrounded the bed on which the deceased lay in state,
and all joined in loud lamentations.

While the grandchildren were singing and participating
in these lamentations, their parents (sons and daughters of
the deceased) would be going up and down the streets, the
men firing guns, and the women singing dirges and wailing.

In the meantime, more and more people from the town,
and from other towns and villages far and near, would have
arrived. As each group came to the house, its members went
around and shook hands with the relatives of the deceased.
And as they shook hands, they expressed their condolences
to each relative for the loss of father (or mother), husband
(or wife), son (or daughter), sister (or brother), uncle, grand-
parent, or grandchild, taking care to give each person's correct relationship to the deceased. Then they were offered
seats, greetings were exchanged, and a blood relative narrated
how the deceased had died; afterward, drinks were served
on behalf of the blood relatives. Those attending the
funeral also gave drinks—or cloth, pillows, or mats for
burying the dead—to the bereaved relatives, or they made
donations of money. These gifts were publicly announced,
and shown to all present. There were fresh outbursts of

weeping and wailing as each new group of sympathizers and mourners arrived, and several bands and drums played throughout.

While this was going on, arrangements were made for digging the grave. Men selected from both the maternal and the paternal relatives were sent to dig the grave. The head of the maternal relatives provided these men with a bottle of rum for the libations to be offered before and at the graveyard. As they set out, they were joined by friends and relatives, who carried their pickaxes, hoes, and cutlasses for them.

If the deceased was to be buried in the family's private grave, only the blood relatives were allowed there; if in a public graveyard, others could go too. In either case, as the company reached the path leading from the main path or road to the place of burial, a son or another blood relative of the deceased offered a libation. Sprinkling three drops of rum on the ground, he called upon God *(Onyakonpon Kwame)* and the Earth *(Asase Yaa)* and the ancestors already buried in the graveyard and informed them that diggers were being sent to make a grave for ——, who had just died. He prayed that his offering of drink would be accepted and that the diggers would be protected from harm while they performed their task.

Then they went to the grave or grayevard, where he offered a libation to the deceased, whose grave was about to be dug, and asked him to help them to complete their task quickly and peacefully. The ground was cleared, and the grave was dug. The relatives would send more drink from the house to the diggers while they were digging the grave. When they had finished, they left their implements at the graveyard and went back to report that the grave was ready.

Burial usually took place a day or two after death, though funeral rites were protracted. There were observances on the eighth, the fifteenth, the fortieth, and the eightieth days after the death, and also on the first anniversary. (These are no longer strictly observed.) Before the body was laid in the coffin, the things—cloths, blankets, pillows, and mats—that had been brought by relatives and friends were shown to those present; those brought by the father of the deceased or his successor were shown first. The head of the maternal relatives usually gave one of his own cloths for the deceased to be buried in. A sum of eight shillings was tied to it. After the things had thus been shown, they were placed beside the corpse, where they were ready to be put into the coffin with it. A gift of three sixpence coins or gold dust was tied to the cloth of the deceased. This was given by a wife or husband or by a blood relative, and it was for the deceased to "buy water" on his journey to the Land of Spirits.

The deceased's nail parings and his hair, which had been cut before the body was bathed, were put in the coffin, together with the towel and sponge and lime that had been used in the bathing. Then the father or his successor sent formally to the head of the maternal relatives to inform him that the body was about to be put into the coffin, and that he should send representatives to see it done. The head of the maternal relatives or his representative was required by custom to be present before the deceased could be put into his coffin. When representatives of both the paternal and maternal groups met, the father of the deceased or his successor poured a libation to the deceased, saying, "We are going to lift you to bury you; go and sleep in peace if you have died as destined; but if not, let us discover who killed you; bring us children; health to all of us; here is drink."

The deceased was put into the coffin, which was then filled with the things that had been given for the burial. The relatives who had tied pieces of one of the deceased's cloths around their necks, heads, wrists, or waists dropped these pieces into the grave (or, occasionally, kept them for the fortieth-day celebration). A fresh burst of wailing and lamentations marked the placing of the body in the coffin. The father of the deceased or his successor led the way; he was followed by the children of the deceased and other relatives, who, in turn, were followed by the coffin bearers; friends, sympathizers, bandsmen, and drummers made up the rear. The bandsmen, drummers, and most of the sympathizers stopped at the path leading to the graveyard. The burial rites themselves were performed without music.

When the grave was reached, the deceased's children took the coffin, and some holding it at the head, others at the feet, they lowered it into the grave. The deceased's father or his father's successor offered another libation; then the deceased's children covered up the grave. The eldest son was the last to stamp on the grave and thus to indicate that he had performed his filial duty—he had buried his father. The Akan says, "I bear a child so that he may hold my head and put me in my grave." Not to have a son to perform this final rite is to have failed in life. When the grave had been covered, the food that was cooked for the deceased was left beside it; a bowl of water was placed with this food.

The procession then returned to the house of mourning. At the entrance to the house, water containing red clay and *adwere* leaves was provided, and everyone dipped his hands into it and sprinkled himself with it before he entered the house. The hoes, cutlasses, and pickaxes that had been used to dig the grave were also sprinkled with this water. This rite was protective as well as purificatory—it was thought to drive away evil spirits. When all had assembled in the house again, the head of the maternal relatives gave drinks to them and, at sundown, begged them to disperse.

The day after the burial, the blood relatives asked all the sympathizers to break their fast. This marked the end of the burial rites, but not of the funeral rites. Akan funerals do not end; the dead are periodically remembered, and their memory is kept always fresh, for they sustain the tribe and its mores.

Culture changes result from choices made between available alternatives. Some alternatives are more quickly accepted than others. Changes in funeral rites are usually among the more strongly resisted ones, for they are bound up with people's views of life and of the universe. The funeral rites described show aspects of Akan culture that have changed little, in spite of the very rapid changes noticeable in other aspects of Akan culture.

In the treatment of the sick, the traditional healer no longer has the field entirely to himself, but he has a surprisingly large part of it. European patent medicines are peddled even in remote villages; clinics, dispensaries, maternity homes, and hospitals, though in inadequate supply, are available; nurses, midwives, and doctors, African and non-African, vie with the traditional healer to bring healing to the sick. The traditional healer has not yet been ousted. He tries to answer questions the others do not answer.

Behind medicine is the universe within which it works, to whose laws it must conform. Body and spirit are parts of a whole. Can health be attained when they are separated? Should they not be treated together? Science is clearly needed, and more and more doctors, and the knowledge and skill they bring. But the continued acceptance of the traditional healer shows that he meets a need—he helps people cope with the problems of their universe. The traditional healer poses a challenge.

3. *Akan Values and the Wider Context of African Cultures*

THE funeral rites of the Akan introduce us to some important features of Akan culture.

Conditions are not idyllic. On the contrary, the people are seen in a grim fight for life. We observe gaps in their scientific knowledge, and we observe the prevalence of disease and human suffering.

But the close-up also shows some fundamental values of the Akan peoples. There is, everywhere, the heavy accent on family—the blood relatives, the group of kinsfolk held together by a common origin and a common obligation to its members, to those who are living and those who are dead. For the family is conceived as consisting of a large number of people, many of whom are dead, a few of whom are living, and countless numbers of whom are yet to be born. The individual is brought up to think of himself always in relation to this group and to behave always in such a way as to bring honor and not disgrace to its members. The ideal set before him is that of mutual helpfulness and cooperation within the group of kinsfolk. Each member should help the other, in health or sickness, in success or failure, in poverty or plenty. We have observed the family constantly around the sick member, and prominent, too, at the funeral rites. There is always the overriding importance of one's membership in the kingroup. There can be no satisfactory or meaningful life for a man except as a member of this group, of his family.

Cooperation and mutual helpfulness are virtues enjoined as essential; without them, the kingroup cannot long endure. Its survival depends on its solidarity. Such a concept of group life makes for warm personal relationships in which every individual has a maximum involvement in the life of the group. This is hardly congruous with life in a large, heterogeneous, competitive society.

When a person reared and prepared emotionally for cooperative life with near kinsfolk is thrust into an impersonal, a severely competitive and acquisitive society, the psychological readjustment demanded of him can be traumatic. For in the kingroup, the emphasis is on helpfulness and generosity, and a member fulfills his obligation not by what he accumulates for himself, but by what he gives to the other members. The donations at funerals and the publicity given to them illustrate ways in which the enjoined virtues of active concern and generosity are encouraged by the group. Esteem and prestige depend on what a member gives to his group.

There is the emphasis on ancestors. Belief in the continuity of the family lies at the basis of obligation, of law and custom, of behavior. It guides and regulates individual conduct. The ancestors continue as members of the group. They watch over it. They reward those who do well, and they punish those who do not fulfill their obligations to the group. For the life of the group, this is an important sanction, ensuring conformity to the mores; for the individual, it is of considerable importance for mental health. Far-reaching consequences can be expected when the solidarity of the group is strained or broken. Its destruction can be a social catastrophe.

Akan funeral rites demonstrate the belief that death is not the end of man, and that it does not sever the links with the kingroup. There is physical separation (ritually symbolized in some of the funerary observances), but the bonds continue. As an Akan epigram puts it, "Blood is indelible."

This points to another value—that placed on human beings. The death of a member is the concern not only of the kingroup but of the whole village or tribal community. Normal activities are stopped; everyone joins in the mourning, in the wailing and drumming and dancing. The cost to the community in time and economic production may be heavy, but the community's values are not measured thus. As stated by a well-known Akan saying, which one may hear in a woman's plaintive dirge at a funeral, "It is man that counts. I call upon gold; it does not answer. I call upon my drapery; there is no answer. It is man that counts. —— has departed. O miserable me."

Man is valued above things. The libation and prayer offered to the newly dead shows that human beings are desired above all else: "Bring us children; health to all of us; here is drink." Life, fertility, abundant life—this is the recurrent burden of most traditional Akan prayers.

Although the foremost desire is for increase in the membership of one's own kingroup, there is recognition of a larger group, a larger family. An Akan epigram teaches that "all belong to one family, though they are separate stalks." But in traditional society, a man's experience of other stalks may be limited to those of the same village or tribe. Neither communications nor ways of earning a living are such as to promote heterogeneity or wide contacts.

The funeral rites also show the elements of Akan religion. There is the predominant emphasis on departed forebears. The ancestors receive constant attention and worship, an acknowledgment of their felt nearness and influence. But libations are poured to the Supreme Being, the Creator of man and of all things, to the gods, who derive their being and powers from him, and to the earth and other natural objects, each of which is conceived as having its own power, which man should seek to propitiate.

We have seen libations poured, heard prayers offered, even to a tree. Yet this reverent attitude did not preclude using the tree's bark to meet a human need. Nature has power, a power that may be useful or harmful; it is safer to appease her. Nature is revered, but when the skill and knowledge are available, she is also used for man's benefit —to serve man's will and purposes.

Is the reverent attitude merely an expression of ignorance of material substances and natural causes? Or of impotence before the immense forces of nature? Or do the rites imply a theory of reality? Behind visible substances, does the Akan find their invisible essence, a power or energy that constitutes their true nature? Something conceived in animistic terms and thus compelling reverence? Until recently, writing was unknown; it is not part of the inherited culture; and such reflections, if any existed, went unrecorded. It is left to posterity to seek the meaning behind the remaining rites and traditions.

Noteworthy, too, is the apparent absence of any conceptual cleavage between the natural and the supernatural. In the search for the causes of an illness, we observed that connections were conceived both in natural and in supernatural terms; physical *and* magical linkages were involved. This is not unimportant to those who are trying to modernize Akan society. If a society is to move from a homogeneous, pretechnical state to a state of heterogeneity and industrialization, it needs minds that understand modern techniques and the kind of thinking that lies behind them. A scientific age demands scientific minds. This is a task of education.

The sense of dependence manifested in Akan rites is also unmistakable. A sense of dependence on God, the

Creator, on lesser deities, on numerous unseen agencies, and on the ancestors. Many powers claim attention, fear, and reverence. Implicit in these claims are assumptions about the character of the universe, about God and man and nature, about the physical and social worlds. It is a universe of spirits.

Knowledge of the physical universe (and the control of nature that comes from such knowledge) has been, as we may deduce from the treatment of disease, manifestly rudimentary. The "diagnosis" and treatment of diseases display large elements of experimentation and guesswork—in which the natural and the supernatural are bewilderingly commingled.

One could select many societies in Africa similar to the Akan, from whose funeral rites we have had a close view of some aspects of a culture in which kinship ties are strong and are manifest in all activities of life. In all of these societies, reverence for the ancestors has a counterpart in the high prestige that the old enjoy in the community. As there is no tradition of writing, the older generations are the educators of the young; the elders are looked up to as those who possess the wisdom and accumulated experience of the tribe, and it is to them that the young turn for instruction and guidance. The introduction of reading and writing into such a society accentuates the gap between the generations and upsets the traditional balance between young and old, for when the young are taught to read and write, new doors to wisdom and knowledge are opened to them. They are no longer dependent on an old man's memory. Formal education has unsuspected consequences for an illiterate community.

The extensive ceremonialism we have observed in Akan funeral rites is another mark of such a culture. Similar rituals surround important seasonal community activities as well as the critical periods of an individual's life. Planting, harvesting, and fishing; birth, puberty, marriage—these are occasions for the community or the kingroup to come together, to join in song and dance or in ritual, to give expression to the sense of group solidarity or the sense of dependence on the ancestors or on other supernatural powers. They are also occasions that provide opportunities for passing on to the young the lore and customs of the community. People can spare the time and be free to participate in these rites because they belong to an agricultural community in which many are self-employed, growing their food on the land that their membership in the kingroup entitles them to use. Increasing productivity is not yet a primary obsession; these people are not yet employees; their time is still their own. Industrialization will set new goals, introduce new values, make new demands. Group solidarity and traditions will be sacrificed as part of the payment for higher standards of living. People will be too busy for long rituals.

This is a reminder that cultures are not static. There is no society so custom-bound that its culture does not change, and there is none so changeful as to have no cake of custom. African cultures are not tied to a golden age in which there can be found, pure and complete, a priceless heritage that has been overlaid by an irreverent scientific age. It is not a question of peering into the past to rediscover the glory that was Africa. Such a conception of Africa fails to take account of the fact that every culture is—at every time—in the process of change. The cultures of African peoples have been growing continuously; they do have their roots in the past, but they stretch into the present, into the happenings of today, and of tomorrow. For culture is built up during man's continuous struggle to reach his goals—in his quest for knowledge to feed and clothe himself, to build his home, to overcome disease, in the way he orders his social life, the ways in which he seeks understanding and a more satisfying fulfillment of his wants. In this process, African peoples have created, learned, borrowed, adapted, accumulated, and added to their cultures, to their material possessions, their institutions, and their ideas.

There have been contacts with other peoples both within and beyond the continent. Within the continent, there have been contacts and exchanges as tribes have moved from one part of Africa to another in search of food, water, or a place where they might live without molestation. Beyond the continent, there have been contacts with different races, interactions that stretch back thousands of years. Through Egypt, Ethiopia, and North Africa came borrowings from the ancient cultures of the Mediterranean; through Madagascar, the ancient cultures of Asia. In more recent times, the violent impact of European cultures has been felt everywhere in Africa.

These various influences have not affected all parts of Africa uniformly, for the degree of contact has varied from place to place. Survivals of extremely old cultures can be found alongside recently borrowed inventions and ideas. The old and the new are both a part of Africa as it is today. The talking drum belongs as much to contemporary African cultures as does the telegraph or the jazz band; the baby at its mother's back as much as the baby in the pram; the lineage or clan as much as the trade union or the political party; the chief as much as the president. All have been accepted and incorporated into the ever-changing and growing cultures that constitute Africa's way of life.

Excessive nationalism should not cause the cultures of Africa to be represented as mysteries that only Africans can understand or share. Any culture can be learned. Africans are a part of mankind, within the stream of human history. They have borrowed inventions, techniques, and ideas from other cultures; and they, too, have contributed to the cultures of other peoples.

What *is* an important factor to reckon with in the study of contemporary African cultures is the fact that, over the centuries, and particularly during the last century and a half, Africans have been overwhelmed by the technological superiority of European cultures and, often, by the political and economic domination of Europeans. This has gravely threatened African cultures, and although it has not destroyed them, it has led to profound changes.

Every culture represents unique answers by a people to certain universal human questions in the context of a particular historical situation, particular resources, skills, and knowledge. Every group finds itself in a natural environment that offers possibilities for, as well as sets limits on, the provision of food, shelter, and clothing, and the fulfillment of other human wants. According to the available knowledge, the group finds its own solutions to the universal problems posed by its basic material needs. These solutions, the answers it adopts, are aspects of its culture—as are the group's solutions to the problems of law and the ordering of human relations in social organizations and political systems, to the problems of human intercourse in language and art, song and dance, and to the problems that grow from man's deeper cravings, his need for mental and spiritual expression in ethics, philosophy, and religion, according to the group's concepts of the universe and man's place and purpose in it. A people's solutions, its answers, are influenced by contacts with other peoples, for such contacts are a part of its experience and knowledge.

African peoples, like others, have borrowed tools and have accepted institutions and ideas which help them in the more efficient control of nature and in the ordering of their affairs. They have accepted new means of communication, new products—food, machines, clothing, other manufactured goods—and new techniques. Each new borrowing or acceptance compels new adjustments, for man's life is lived as a whole, and his culture is an equilibrium of functionally interrelated parts. Each new borrowing or acceptance enriches the culture, but it has to be fitted into the whole.

Comparatively little is known of the past cultures of Africa. A great deal has still to be learned, or reconstructed, from oral tradition, from ethnological and archaeological studies, and from such historical sources as are available. Studies that are going on are revealing more and more about the past cultures. But Africa is a large continent, and assertions about it are too often made on the basis of a single community or a small geographical area.

One talks of African cultures, for the different communities have had different historical and social experiences, which are reflected in different cultures. Yet, by comparing studies of different African communities, it is possible to discern certain similarities—similarities in funeral rites, in dances, in religion, social organization, and attitudes toward nature. In particular, studies of the art and music of different African communities (growing art collections are being analyzed and interpreted in museums in Africa, Europe, America, and other parts of the world) show distinctive characteristics in terms of form, rhythm, emotion, structure, symbolism. In comparison with the art or music of other countries, these characteristics are peculiarly African. Even when all of these characteristics are present, however, specialists can often identify a work of art or a musical piece as belonging to a particular African area or tribe. There are differences as well as similarities. Published symposia on African languages, political organization, kinship systems, and religion, for example, have shown different cultural patterns; some of the differences are quite profound.

From available information, attempts have been made

by scholars to map out culture areas on the basis of selected patterns of culture. The research and comparative studies continue. Without severe limitations and clearly specified items of comparison, the term "African culture," as pertaining to a way of life uniformly applicable to the whole continent, has little, if any, precise sociological meaning.

Today, there are more opportunities than ever before for Africans from different parts of the continent to meet and to test in their own experience what others write about them. When they meet, they cannot fail to see that they do not belong to one all-embracing culture. Obvious differences, of language, dress, customs, exist alongside obvious similarities, common interests and experiences, shared aspects of culture. The fact of belonging geographically to the same continent (neither race nor color is uniform throughout Africa) does not make Africans develop the same cultural patterns in all spheres of human activity. In accordance with particular historical situations and particular experiences, Africans have given different answers to universal as well as particular questions.

There is, at the present time, a quest by Africans for unity and cooperation on a wider scale than has hitherto been possible. Consequently, attempts have been made to find bases for unity in conceptual formulations. The most prominent of these attempts have given expression to the concepts of African personality and Negritude.

There are wide individual differences among human beings, even among those who belong to the same country and are brought up in the same culture. In a sense, every human being is a unique personality, never completely duplicated. Nonetheless, in sociological and psychological studies, as well as in popular judgment, it is assumed that the members of any one organized, relatively permanent group, such as a nation, manifest personality traits and characteristics that distinguish them from the members of other similar groups. Thus Africans may be contrasted with Americans or Indians or Chinese, with Frenchmen or with Englishmen.

When personality is considered as a product of the social environment, it is supposed that those who have shared the same social tradition will manifest in their individual personalities elements that may be described as culturally regular—i.e., as common to all those who have been integrated into the given social tradition. Thus nationals of a sovereign political state are expected personally to embody "national" elements of the culture in which they have been reared. These elements are thought to be correlates of a shared citizenship and of such things as a common language, common economic, political, educational, and religious institutions, moral codes, traditions—correlates, that is, of socio-cultural factors that, taken together, are said to affect the personality organization of the individual members of the nation. The common set of conditions and experiences is expected to produce some common general traits and characteristics—thus, national character.

The concept of national character is an abstraction serving, in any given instance, to embody a set of culturally regular traits. The concept of African personality belongs in the same category as that of national character; it, too, is an abstraction embodying a set of culturally regular traits said to be exhibited by nationals who have been integrated into a shared social tradition. But the difficulty becomes at once apparent. What is the shared social tradition with reference to which the abstraction of an African personality is conceived? Where does it prevail? In the whole continent? In parts of the continent? Which parts? In terms of culture, as has been indicated, there is not one social tradition; there are different social traditions. And there are different nationalities.

The concept of African personality is of recent origin and is really an expression of political aspirations. In a negative sense, it is a reaction to colonialism. It is a protest against European domination and the crude biological theories that have been used in efforts to justify European imperialism. In this sense, as will be shown, the concept is an expression of nationalism. As a protest against colonialism or imperialism, it has a wide appeal, for colonial subjection is an experience in which many African peoples have shared.

The concept is also a reaction against the disdain that has been shown for African cultures and the stunting they have suffered under European domination, and against the enthronement, conscious and unconscious, of the cultures of imperialist countries. In this sense, the concept of African personality is a claim to and an assertion of cultural freedom. The wearing of traditional attire and the appreciation and encouragement of once neglected traditional art, music, dance, and religion—this too is an aspect of nationalism. It marks an effort to rediscover Africa's social heritage. It is demanded by national pride. It is a search for roots, for self-confidence.

And more, the concept of African personality is an arbitrary focusing of common sentiments in an emotional appeal for the unity of African states. It provides an emotional basis for the political aspiration toward establishment of a "United States of Africa."

In the last analysis, the concept of African personality is a political myth; but for that reason it can have a strong emotional appeal and profound social consequences. There have already been extravagant abuses of the concept. It has been appealed to to justify undemocratic practices and ruthless steps toward the establishment of one-party rule, and to excuse such patent injustices as the arbitrary arrest of political figures and their imprisonment without trial. Blatant aggressiveness has been defended as the projection of the African personality. But these clear aberrations are not necessarily inherent in the concept, either as a protest against colonialism or as a defense of cultural freedom.

The concept of Negritude represents a philosophical approach, although it, too, is a revolt against imperialism. In particular, it is a revolt against the French policy toward African cultures, a policy that has completely ignored them, on the assumption that, because French culture represents a "higher" civilization, the best thing would be for France's African subjects to adopt the culture of their rulers. The concept of Negritude has thus been promulgated by African intellectuals of former French colonies—principally, by Alioune Diop and Léopold Sédar Senghor.

Senghor's approach is in line with the concept of national character as explained above. He sees Negritude as a pair of common psychic traits possessed by the Negro African— "his heightened sensibility and his strong emotional quality." "Emotion is Negro." The concept of Negritude may be regarded as a convenient abstraction, a conceptual tool for researchers who are trying to find common cultural traits that will distinguish the Negro African from other races. But "heightened sensibility" and "strong emotional quality"— those cannot be claimed as the exclusive possessions of Negro Africans, nor as qualities embodied in every Negro African irrespective of his cultural heritage and social experience. The essential problem of the concept is that race and culture do not necessarily go together. People of different races have belonged to the same culture, and people of the same race have belonged to different cultures. Historical circumstances have put Negro Africans into different cultures, and the personality traits conditioned by these cultures cannot be assumed to be identical. Even if they were, it should be noted that the concept of Negritude would express values common to only one of the races of Africa. For not all Africans are Negro Africans.

Diop conceives of Negritude as the values that are the "vindication of the dignity of persons of African descent." His position is understandable against the background of French colonial policy. And all "persons of African descent" are not Negroes.

The concept of Negritude thus requires further clarification and refinement. It can, however, be seen as a *quest* for the "vindication of the dignity of persons of African descent," as a quest of Africans for recognition as equals in a world-wide brotherhood of man.

This puts the question of African cultures in the perspective of contemporary history, which is where it belongs. The challenge to African cultures is the challenge to the spirit of man to meet the new situations in which man must try to fulfill his goals and aspirations. It is the challenge of the battle of life.

African communities of the past, according to their opportunities and lights, and within their limitations, created the heritages that present generations enjoy—or are seeking to rediscover. In part, the challenge of the contemporary situation is being met in the learning, choices, acceptances, rejections, and adaptations of cultures that have come to accept new goals—the conquest of disease, of poverty and ignorance, the sharing of wider human relationships, in larger groupings, outside Africa as well as within it. Many adjustments are made necessary by the increasing interdependence of peoples, by the very need for survival in this highly technological age—this atomic age. These are the challenges Africans face. They must establish new institutions. Their cultures must change and grow, but they must retain that identification with the past which gives every people its sense of uniqueness and pride.

Other peoples face the same challenges. Africans belong to the stream of human history. Their cultures must be viewed against the background of contemporary history. And a prominent and inescapable factor of that background is the impact of Europe on Africa, to which we turn in the next section.

II

*THE CHALLENGE
OF COLONIAL EXPERIENCE*

4. The Invasion of Technology

IT is interesting in the study of history to note how a practice that is carried on without compunction or disapproval in one era is condemned and abhorred in another. Mankind does make moral progress.

Colonialism is in general disfavor today, so much so, that it has become a tactic of certain political leaders to level the charge of colonialism (or that of imperialism) against countries they seek to discredit. Colonialism is regarded as something to be ashamed of, and not only is it condemned, but there are countries that manifest a sense of guilt about it. The development of these attitudes is itself of interest, historically, as well as psychologically.

Both attitudes are understandable, for colonialism has been associated with international wars, with slavery, and with some of the worst examples of man's inhumanity to man. But that is not the whole picture. Colonialism is important historically. It is impossible to understand our contemporary society without considering its impact. One has only to think of countries like the United States, Canada, New Zealand, Australia, India, Burma, and Ceylon, all former British colonies, to realize what a force colonialism has been in the creation of the international society of the twentieth century.

Colonialism drew Africa into the orbit of modern history. During 1961, rioting and fighting in Algeria, tragic events in the Congo, and more recently, the stark drama of atrocities in Portuguese Angola, have been sharp and shocking reminders that colonialism does not belong to the past only, but continues into the present. Situations such as those in Angola, from where there are continuous reports of oppression, torture, and massacre, heighten and justify the sense of indignation, and grievance, that rankles in many minds whenever colonialism is mentioned. For colonialism will continue to be a threat to peaceful relations among nations until its inevitable end comes.

The invectives against imperialism and colonialism lead to frequent accusations against colonial powers, and to equally spirited defenses. In the charges and countercharges leveled in these acrimonious exchanges, the reasons and motives for the colonization of Africa by European powers have been debated over and over again, often with more heat and emotion than desire to find out the truth.

It has been frequently stressed that the industrialization of Europe created a need for markets, and that this was the principal reason for the colonization of Africa. The facts support the view that during the period from 1870 to 1910, economic developments in Europe led to an intensification of the rivalry among European powers for colonies in Africa. But a historical event that involved so many countries and peoples can quite reasonably be expected to have had more than one cause or motive. And reasons and motives other than the need for markets have, in fact, been advanced.

One interesting theory concerning the "scramble for Africa" (as the rivalry for African colonies in the latter part of the nineteenth century has been aptly described) sought to justify the colonial wars waged against African peoples on the basis of the then highly fashionable social application of Darwin's theory of evolution. Professor Karl Pierson, for example, asserted, in *National Life from the Standpoint of Science* (published in 1900): "History shows me one way, and one way only, in which a state of civilization has been produced, namely, the struggle of race with race, and the survival of the physically and mentally fitter race." According to this, the conquests in Africa were justified on the basis of the biological theory that it was the fittest species that survived in the struggle for existence. Europeans triumphed over Africans because the former belonged to a "fitter" race. This sort of notion has been the bane of international relations ever since.

The victories of Europeans were easy to explain on other grounds. Since many tribes in West, East, and Central Africa fought with bows and arrows, spears, or, at best, muskets against Europeans armed with rifles and cannon, it is clear that the "fitness" of the Europeans lay in their technology rather than biology. Their technical superiority ensured their military successes.

The justification of colonial wars on the basis of Darwinian—hence, scientific—theory may have salved consciences or satisfied national pride. It certainly encouraged and it very probably added support for the jingoism that marked the period when it was most popular. But it does not appear to have taken account of the many, and protracted, wars that different countries of Caucasoid Europe fought with each other. In fact, the story of the colonization of Africa is, on the one hand, the story of the relations between different European powers of the Caucasoid race, as rivals and competitors for colonies, and on the other, of the impact these powers have had on the African countries they colonized. The theory that implied innate inequalities among races has not been supported by the findings of students of human biology.

 — Another interesting motive for the colonization of Africa was stated by H. H. Wyatt at the time when colonialism was at the height of its popularity. In his book *Ethics of Empire* (published in 1897), Wyatt, with special reference to Britain's empire building, wrote: "To us [i.e., the British] and not to others, a certain definite duty has been assigned: to carry light and civilization into the dark places of the world, to touch the mind of Asia and of Africa with the ethical ideas of Europe, to give to thronging millions who would otherwise never know peace and security, these first conditions of human advance." Every colonial African territory has a long catalogue of instances that suggest Wyatt's kind of idealism be greeted with some skepticism. Yet it has to be allowed that there have been individuals, and associations, whom a sense of mission, or ideals of the kind stated by Wyatt, drew from Europe to Africa in the colonial period. It is also a fact that there are many in Africa who owe their education to nationals of European colonizing powers; to that extent, many minds have been uplifted. Individual motivations and national policies are, of course, not the same; both must be considered in appraising the effects of colonialism. The impact of colonialism on the minds of the peoples of the countries that were colonized must be taken account of in any objective assessment of the results of the colonization of Africa.

In his *Dual Mandate in British Tropical Africa* (published in 1926), Lord Lugard expounded the colonial trusteeship theory. This was really similar in approach to the suggestion that British colonization was inspired by a sense of mission. The trusteeship theory stated that Britain had a dual obligation toward its colonies: first, to help the colonial peoples to advance, and second, to develop the resources of the colonies for the benefit of mankind generally.

Two theories have been of special interest politically. One of these identifies colonialism with capitalist exploitation, an identification that follows the Marxist analysis of colonialism. (Stalin, for example, viewed the British Empire in terms of the oppression and exploitation of subject races by the doomed capitalists of Great Britain.) Colonialism is represented as a consequence of capitalist expansion, its aim and result being the exploitation and impoverishment of the subject peoples of the colonies. This theory has had great appeal in Africa, for it provides material for protests against the injustices of commercial and political domination.

The second theory that has affected political policies is the racial one. The theory of innate superiority of certain races and innate inferiority of others has been advanced in various forms to explain or justify colonialism, whether by the French, the British, the Belgians, or the Portuguese. Although authoritative pronouncements have been made by eminent scientists saying that there is no evidence to support this theory, it has continued to influence national policies and practices in Africa.

These theories show that different reasons and motives for the colonization of Africa have been offered. Quarrels and arguments about them continue. In a subject like this, it is possible to select facts to support one theory or another, according to personal predilection. A reflection on the vacillations of Britain's policies toward its colonies in Africa between 1870 and 1910 gives one the impression that there was more than a jest in Sir John Seeley's assertion that the British "conquered and peopled half of the world in a fit of absence of mind." His book on *The Expansion of England,* in which this statement appeared, was published in 1833, before the "scramble for Africa" really began, but it is relevant to the theories that seek to give reasons or motives for the colonization of Africa. It brings home the notable lesson that such explanations of historical events are often insights or hindsights of other people, ascribing designs and motives that were not clearly perceived by those who enacted the events.

The reasons and motives for the colonization of Africa

were mixed; the desire for markets was among them, as was the idea of national prestige, as were concepts of altruistic idealism. But the driving force for the acquisition of possessions in Africa by European powers in the last quarter of the nineteenth century came chiefly from the growing industrialization of Europe and the need for markets and raw materials to which this industrialization gave rise. The colonization of Africa and the industrialization of Europe were closely linked, and the recognition of that link is important for understanding the African situation. Everywhere in Africa one encounters industrial products, machinery, and power tools that testify to the technological superiority of Europe—and to the degree to which European technology has invaded the entire life of the peoples of Africa.

Colonialism is, above all, a social fact. It is essentially a situation involving human relations. The colonization of Africa by European powers brought African peoples into contact with peoples who had ways of life different from their own.

Contacts between human beings evoke mutual responses, and the peoples of Africa have responded to the incursions of colonial powers in every aspect of their lives—economic, political, social, religious, and also aesthetic. Consequently, there has been culture change. From the relationships and social changes that came into being during the period of colonization, contemporary Africa has emerged.

The most notable and impressive lesson was that of the power of Europe, a power based on superior technology. It is an unforgettable lesson. Older Africans, those who fought in the wars against European countries, when asked about their most vivid impressions of the wars, invariably say, "The white man is powerful."

Superior arms brought home that lesson, but commerce

and trade have also attested to it. Imported foods and clothing can be found in the remotest villages of Africa. The hoe and the cutlass, which are still in use on African farms, are imported from Europe; more recently, the plow, the tractor, and the bulldozer have made their way into the once impenetrable forests. Bicycles, motor cars, railways, the telegraph, the telephone, radio, and even television have revolutionized the means of communication; new building materials, gas and electric stoves, washing machines and refrigerators, and the air conditioner are setting new standards for the African home.

The invasion is uneven. Some areas have felt its impact to a much greater degree than others. The remote village has felt it less than the commercial town, the harbor, or the industrial or mining town. Its impact on persons has also been uneven. The farmer, for example, has felt it less than the Western-educated professional man; nevertheless, both have felt it.

The products of European technology are a part of the Africa of today, which bears the indelible marks of their impact. An important consequence of the colonization of Africa is the technical progress it has made possible. Some would make this concession grudgingly; they would point out that Europeans have used their technical superiority to gain and maintain possessions in Africa—that the roads, railways, telephones, and telegraph have helped them to rule more effectively, and to expand their trade; that through the sale of the industrial goods produced by their technology, they have been able to make colonial subjects adopt a European way of life, which again is good for trade; that the printed word, the cinema, and the radio are all instruments for influencing men's minds so that they may become better customers and consumers of European goods. There is much truth in all this. Yet it must also be remembered that there has been technical progress.

It would not be altogether correct to conclude that technical progress has been forced on Africa. Much of it has been willingly chosen and accepted. All peoples welcome technological advances, for, through them, men gain knowledge that can increase their efficiency and their ability to bend their physical environment to the more effective service of their wants. Man's desire everywhere is to master nature and to make it serve him. The transport, trade, and industry that Europe has introduced to Africa have been accepted because of the contributions they make to the improvement of life. The evidence is that more and more technical progress is needed—and desired.

The growth of technology has played an important role in the history of mankind. Not only has it caused social revolutions within countries, but it has profoundly affected the relations between countries. As was the case between Africa and Europe in the last century, superior technology has decided military conquests and, therefore, the relations between nations. The struggle for power among nations, and between classes within nations, is bound up with the growth of technology.

The factors that cause social change are complex, and it is seldom that a particular phenomenon of social or cultural change can be wholly attributed to one factor; but in considering the challenge of colonialism, the social and cultural adaptations African communities have made to the technology of Europe demand attention. In this context, we include the responses made to the products of the European industrial revolution as these products have been introduced into Africa from the nineteenth century to the present day. Industrial agriculture, mining, transportation, communications, the production of textiles, the use of power engines and machine tools, of electricity and chemicals—all of these, and all of the processes and techniques connected with them, have helped to impel the social and cultural revolution of Africa.

The nature of the revolution is best seen against the background of the rapidly changing indigenous cultures of Africa. There are differences in these cultures, but underlying the specific diversities, are certain similarities. A few generalizations may be made. Indigenous African societies are kin-bound societies. The account of the treatment of the sick and of funeral rites given in the previous chapter shows how paramount kinship solidarity can be in such situations. Studies of many African societies have emphasized the important role that is played by the kinship organizations.

All activities of social life, economic, political, and religious, are based on kinship relations. In the economic sphere, the traditional system of production and distribution is based on reciprocities that derive from the complex web of ties that links kinsfolk. Similarly, in the political sphere, rights and obligations, inheritances, the succession to public office, and the maintenance of order are all based on kinship structures. The success of community life depends on the solidarity of local groups of kinsfolk. A focus on what is happening to the kinship structures should, therefore, throw light on the social revolution that is taking place in Africa. Social strains accompany culture contacts, and the strains on the institution of the family reflect the changes these contacts have wrought in Africa.

There are variants in the patterns of kinship organization. Within kingroups are the domestic units of kinsmen who share the same homestead. These domestic groupings vary from the monogamous household, which consists of husband, wife, and their unmarried children, to the polygamous family, in which each of two or more wives constitutes, with her children, a separate unit; from the extended paternal family, in which a man lives in the same household with his married sons and their wives, to the matrilocal domestic group that consists of a wife, her husband, and their daughters and their husbands. The type of houses, the way in which they are grouped, and the number of rooms provided are, in the traditional setting, dictated by the pattern of the domestic unit. An African village or town is thus in conformity with the social organization. In present circumstances, this kind of situation does not obtain in the mining or commercial towns, where houses have been provided without regard to traditional patterns. The new towns have grown to meet new needs, and housing like that which is offered in these towns has been one of the insidious ways in which traditional kinship structures have been attacked.

Another feature common to African societies is that, whatever the pattern or size of the domestic unit, the range of relationships recognized for effective social life extends beyond that unit to include other kinsfolk—descendants of a common ancestress in those tribes where the emphasis is on maternal descent; of a common ancestor, where the emphasis is on paternal descent. A man's obligations are to a wider group than his elementary family. It used to be thought, and even asserted authoritatively, that town life and education created a "detribalized" African, whose ties with the wider kingroups were broken. More intensive studies have caused this view to be modified. One of the problems of social change, as far as it concerns the individual African, is the problem of meeting his felt and accepted kinship obligations in entirely new economic circumstances.

Still another common feature of African societies is that marriage is an integral part of the extended kinship structure. For marriage is not only a socially recognized bond between two persons, but it is also a socially recognized bond between two kingroups, upon which it imposes new reciprocal obligations and duties. Thus the shift toward emphasizing marriage as primarily a bond between two persons is yet another insidious, and serious, way in which African social structures have been attacked.

Kinship structures are buffeted from many sides. The economies of African societies have been described as subsistence economies. The available technological equipment and skills enable the people to do little more than meet their essential needs for food, shelter, and clothing. Even this requires the joint efforts of the domestic unit. Production and distribution often take in a wider group of kinsmen.

Farm work, hunting, and fishing are cooperative ventures. There is division of labor on the basis of sex, but opportunities for differentiation and specialization are hardly available. Whether what is produced is meager or plentiful, there is an obligation to provide for all members of the household or kingroup, even if this can be done only on the basis of subsistence standards of living. The stereotype of Africa as a land where nature provided so abundantly that man had little need to work, where man was, in consequence, perennially lazy, was long ago shattered by anthropological studies of the economies of African peoples in different parts of the continent, north, south, east, west, and central.

But romanticism dies hard. The truth is that, over vast areas of Africa, the challenge of natural conditions and habitat is so severe, and technology is so inadequate and inefficient, that whole families have to work hard all the year round to provide for a bare subsistence. By increasing man's ability to cope with his environment, technical progress makes it possible for him to provide himself with more than what is required for mere subsistence. In fact, one of the problems of interest to all Africa is what has been termed "the challenge of environment"—the challenge of poor soils, of harsh climate, of uncertain and inadequate food supplies, and of disease.

The common need is the need for development. Experience of colonialism has shown that development is possible through the application of science and technology. It has shown new possibilities in the fight with nature; poverty, ignorance, and disease can be fought with greater hope. In this context, colonialism has achieved at least two things. First, European powers have laid the foundations for economic growth. It can be shown that many African colonies and ex-colonies are still sorely deficient in public utilities—harbors, roads, railways, telecommunications, and the like. And it can be shown that standards of living are low. But it can also be shown that the European imperial powers have laid a foundation for economic growth by providing some of the utilities and services that are prerequisites of development. Everywhere, some public utilities (such as roads, railways, harbors, water supplies, irrigation, telecommunications), some public services (medical care, for example, or schools), and some productive enterprises (mines, plantations, or factories) have been provided. They mark the invasion of European technology and the products and skills associated with it.

Second, colonialism has shown Africa new possibilities of human achievement in the battle against poverty, ignorance, and disease. Paradoxically, this has also served to inspire the overthrow of colonialism—in order that the achievements colonial powers have shown to be possible, but dawdle over, may the more quickly be realized. The contrast between what is thought to be possible and what is actually provided or achieved under colonial rule has heightened the sense of indignation at the injustice of colonialism and, hence, the determination to end colonial rule. Technology made colonial rule possible; increasing awareness of what is attainable through technology increases the opposition to colonialism.

What has been achieved under colonial rule also confirms the fact that development requires changes in social institutions, in habits, and in values. Whatever the political machinery—capitalist, socialist, or communist, dictatorial or democratic—fundamental changes occur in the structure and functioning of a society invaded by new technology. For the invasion of technology affects all aspects of social life.

Although technology is usually considered in relation to man's physical environment, it is essentially social rather than physical. One aspect of the colonization of Africa is the effect of European technology on African societies. The transformation of the economy; the growth of towns and of heterogeneity in them; changes in the institutions of family, kingroup, and clan, and in the structure of society generally; better communications, improved health, and newly developed public services; effective government exercised over wider areas—all of these derive from the invasion of technology and link the colonial past with the present, with the rapid changes, the lofty aspirations, and the challenges with which contemporary Africa is grappling.

An objective historical review of colonialism will confirm that there was more than one motive for the colonization of Africa, and that along with this colonization, came the invasion of technology. But such a review cannot disguise the fact that colonialism rests on force and injustice—or the fact that its persistence constitutes the most burning challenge in Africa today.

5. The Impact of European Government and Administration

T
HE emergent nations of Africa have all been under the political control of one European nation or another. They share a common sentiment born of the common experience of domination by an alien power. Nevertheless, there are differences. The European powers that colonized Africa adopted different policies and evolved different administrative systems in the pursuit of their different objectives. The British have frequently insisted that their policy was to train the subject peoples of their colonies for self-government. When one examines French colonial policy, one discerns running through it a conception of some kind of union between metropolitan France and its colonies. Belgian policy has been aptly summarized by G. Malengreau, himself a Belgian and an authority on the subject (in an article he wrote for a conference held in Washington, in 1954, under the auspices of Johns Hopkins University, and published in *Africa Today*), as one of "patient empiricism." It is a policy that has been marked by concentration on economic development rather than on training colonial subjects for political responsibility. The policy of Portugal has been to regard its African colonies as extensions of the Portuguese mainland, a policy emphasized by designating the colonies

POL

as "provinces" of Portugal. As for Spain, what is apparent in its colonial policy is the close economic integration of the African colonies with metropolitan Spain. There has been little indication what the political future of Spain's colonies will be. The Republic of South Africa has left no doubt that its policy is to maintain white domination.

Different policies and objectives led to the establishment of different administrative and bureaucratic systems. In consequence, some colonial subjects have enjoyed more freedom than others, or have had greater opportunities for advancement. Colonial rule has not meant the same thing all over Africa.

But one characteristic *is* common to all colonial systems: all have been authoritarian. All the new nations of Africa have inherited a legacy of authoritarian political structures from their former rulers. This is a fact worthy of note, especially in relation to the political institutions that are being developed by the nationalist governments that have succeeded colonial rulers.

An eminent Africanist (testifying before an official committee of his government in 1960) stated, *inter alia:* "It is reasonable to assume that, in the immediate future, we shall see governments with powers vested in a strong executive, and where one-party systems predominate, if only because of the need to mobilize resources and labor for development along a line which is inimical to the process of debate that in the two-party and multi-party systems must precede decisions as to policies and their implementation." He went on to caution that "African one-party systems are not to be equated with totalitarianism." He might have pointed out that the administrative structures that nationalist governments inherit at independence are bureaucracies in which powers are vested in executives with no tradition of party government or opposition.

There is an element of continuity in the situation. Co-

lonial governments are not democratic governments. They
are not based on consent. Each is the embodiment of the
power of an alien country. A colonial government demands
obedience; its laws must be obeyed. Those who represent
the metropolitan country are top administrators and law-
givers, not subject to the will of those whom they rule. They
require not that their colonial subjects acquiesce, but that
they submit. Accordingly, the administrative structure devised is such as can be used for the effective exercise of
authority by the few who are directly appointed by a metropolitan country to rule, on its behalf, the many who are
indigenous to the colony. It is important to grasp this point
in order to appreciate the current tendencies in Africa.

The development of "strong executives" has also been
encouraged by investors who insist that, as a guarantee for
the security of their investments, they require strong, stable
governments, about which they have shown more concern
than about the civil liberties of the governed. An African
leader who set out resolutely to establish a "strong government" by the ruthless elimination of opposition justified his
conduct by saying that he wanted investments, and investors
did not ask whether there were civil liberties or whether
there was an opposition party in his country, but whether
there was stability and a strong leader capable of ensuring
its maintenance. Indeed, a strong opposition that offered
itself as an alternative government and commanded sufficient
popular support to constitute a threat to the party in power
was deemed to be a disability. The government could not be
regarded as stable.

Investors demand "strong" governments, governments
with large and comfortable majorities and with "strong"
men at their head, governments that can safely be expected
to remain in the saddle. Hence some African leaders have
been encouraged to believe that it is wise to maintain the
authoritarian traditions of former colonial powers—and

wiser still to improve on them in the direction of totalitarianism, thus reassuring would-be investors. When this has been done, investments have poured in. The investors in question were themselves citizens of Western democracies, where they enjoyed and cherished their civil liberties, and where vigorous parties offered alternative governments to the electorates. One such investor explained, "If we were to ask for democratic systems before we invested, there would be very few areas in the world for our investments." All the new nations need investments, and this insidious demand of investors for "strong" governments should not be lightly discounted.

African one-party systems may not be totalitarian in the beginning—no more so than the colonial governments they succeed. But it should be recognized (as some African leaders have already shown) that they inherit political machinery easily adaptable to totalitarianism. Colonial governments themselves, however, excepting that they do not rest on contractual agreement, conform remarkably (in the best instances) to Hobbes's picture of the state, which has a strong executive, but in which, nevertheless, the subjects have "the liberty to buy and sell, and otherwise contract with one another, to choose their own abode, their own diet, their own trade of life, and institute their children as they themselves think fit, and the like." This represents a more lenient authoritarianism than is allowed in some African colonies, for there are areas in Africa where Africans are not permitted "to choose their own abode" or "their own trade of life." But, on the whole, colonial governments are not totalitarian; they do not regulate and control every aspect of life, though the extent of freedom varies under different colonial powers.

However, all colonial governments can be characterized as authoritarian. For a colonial government exists in its own right, by virtue of conquest or power, and its superiority entitles it to demand obedience, which is not derived from the will or the interests of the colonial subjects it rules. As was shown in the previous chapter, and as will become evident in subsequent chapters, benefits have resulted from colonial rule; nevertheless, the essential character of colonial administration is authoritarian. The master commands; the servant must obey. Clearly, such a situation could not forever remain unchallenged.

Po L

⌈African communities, or tribes, developed their own political systems before the period of colonization. Every society must have its own institutions for the maintenance of social order and the control and regulation of the use of physical force. With special reference to Africa, indigenous political organizations also gave emphasis to the settlement of disputes and the restoration of harmonious personal relations, on which the communities placed a high value. Some communities and tribes (the Bemba of Northern Rhodesia, the Ngwato of the Bechuanaland Protectorate, the Ashanti of Ghana, the Yoruba of Nigeria, the Zulu of South Africa, to mention only a few examples) had highly developed political organizations, with differentiated hierarchies of officeholders, from kings and chiefs to attendants, wielding varying degrees of authority. Each organization was one in which different individuals played different roles. The significant thing was that everyone had a role, and everyone had some degree of participation in political life; for political organization was an aspect of the social life, in which everyone participated.⌋

Colonial rule meant the superimposition of a new bureaucracy. Indigenous political systems were either destroyed or radically modified. One general result to which attention may be called was the divorce of many people in villages, as well as in towns, from participation in local government and local decisions. Even where, as in British territories, indigenous political organizations were used, the roles were significantly changed. Chiefs and their councils became subject to the authority and direction of district commissioners or agents representing the imperial power, rather than to the will of their own people. The people were expected not to initiate, but to obey. The psychological result was the breeding of inertia in the general populace, which learned to expect government to do everything. Initiative lay with the imperial officers and their representatives.

Destruction of the sense of civic responsibility is one of the most striking effects of direct rule by an alien power. At independence, it presents to the leaders of the new nation one of their most formidable problems. Without the active and massive participation of the people, it is impossible to carry out the required tasks of nation building and development. But the populace has to be roused from the stupor into which it has been thrown by years of political domination, years during which power has been so centralized in the hands of imperial officials that the people have had little share in deciding even on the local matters that touch their own lives. The legacy of impressive central legislatures and bureaucratic machinery very often has no base in local communities, and presents only a deceptive façade of political progress.

Africa's indigenous political institutions were responsive to the local needs of their communities, though there were few that served large and heterogeneous groups. Generally, there was little need for formal controls, though some tribes had recognized procedures and established penal sanctions for dealing with offenses. Neither police force (or its equivalent) nor full-time administrative cadre was employed. The necessary services were provided as a part of one's civic obligations, and in most cases, the direct expression of public sentiment was a sufficient sanction to restrain wrongdoers.

Colonial governments brought together tribes and chiefdoms that were once separate, or even at loggerheads with one another, and dealt with them in larger administrative units. New administrative structures were built up to accommodate the diverse tribes and groups that were thus brought together. In the new machinery of government, the full-time administrator, the policeman, the soldier, and the civil servant made their appearance.

Not only was there a new administrative structure, but there was also a new conception of the functions of government, a conception illustrated by the building of roads, police stations, military quarters, hospitals, and the like. Foundations were being laid for modern states, which, if they are to function successfully and effectively, must have adequate structures, including roads and schools, civil servants, and police. The tasks were begun, and had to be carried forward when independence came.

Often one of the first tasks to be accomplished when independence is gained, is to complete the structure begun by colonial powers—to build a nation out of the different groups colonialism has brought together. For an administrative framework provides neither an inner unity nor the sentiment of nationhood. It points the way, and helps toward it, just as do the greater physical contacts that new and improved communications make possible.

But in Africa, group and tribal ties are still strong. As has been shown, group solidarity was the essential foundation of social life. It is an interesting phenomenon that certain words in the course of time become loaded with irrational emotions and prejudices. "Tribalism" is one such word. "Tribe" and "tribalism" have become so readily and prejudicially equated with whatever is reactionary that few pause to give any further examination to the matter.

Constitutional problems that have appeared in different African countries (in Ghana, Nigeria, the Belgian Congo, Uganda, and Northern Cameroons, among others) have consistently shown that indigenous, or tribal, groups wish to maintain their political identity. Indigenous groups have often refused to exchange European domination for what they fear may be similar control by other indigenous groups. Appropriate constitutional devices to accommodate this fact have been demanded. Some countries have tried to meet it by federal or regional constitutional arrangements; others have regarded it as a reactionary tendency to be crushed by strong measures.

Among the tribal groups that have demanded constitutional arrangements in recognition of their group solidarity are the Ashanti of Ghana, the Yoruba and the Ibo of Nigeria, and the Baganda of Uganda. Far from being reactionary groups, they are among the most progressive in Africa, and their respective accomplishments give evidence of civic maturity as developed as can be found in any African community. This compels scrutiny of the assumptions that tribalism is reactionary and necessarily incompatible with nationhood.

When the demands of kingdoms or confederations of chiefdoms are described as "tribalism," the term should be explained; otherwise, it gives rise to misconceptions and to misunderstanding of the real problem. In the instances above, the demands made can be seen as expressions of a desire for political participation and control of local affairs to an extent denied by the authoritarian structures of the colonial regimes—and the even more authoritarian ones that threaten to supersede them. Where, as in many of the new African states, there are no institutional checks or established traditions against authoritarianism, the decentralization of political power on the basis of regions or communities offers one way of providing safeguards against political tyranny, against the personality cult and other totalitarian phenomena that tend to become manifest. The administrative machinery of colonial regimes, which is so easily adaptable to oppressive and even totalitarian control, may well require loosening where democracy and civil liberties are prized; and in this context, the demands for regional autonomy, for community or tribal identity, and for greater participation in and control of local affairs, all of which have been labeled as "tribalism" and condemned as reactionary, may represent greater foresight and civic maturity than detractors allow.

The general problem is that the administrative structure of a colonial regime, being authoritarian, does not allow sufficiently for local participation or control; it is super-imposed upon rather than integrated with local communities. Democratic government requires a different structure. And this is one of the challenges the new nations must face.

Stemming from colonial rule are the problems of the impact of European law, its underlying concepts, and its implicit assumptions on the new nations of Africa. Legal associations and experts have, in recent years, given deserved attention to these problems. When European colonial powers brought different communities together, they introduced laws for the heterogeneous groups. Before that time, indigenous political organizations individually decided upon what can properly be called legal matters. Each territorial community provided for the settlement of disputes among its members, the award of just satisfaction to those who suffered injury, the restoration of personal relationships strained or broken by a wrong; directly or indirectly, it provided also for the application of penal sanctions.

Studies of different African communities have shown that some had well-organized political systems with recognized procedures and judicial institutions; others met their judicial needs by spontaneous, collective, but nonetheless, clearly institutionalized action. Under European rule, people from different tribes, observing different customs, came to live in the same town or village, or within the same administrative unit. Europeans lived alongside Africans. Trade and commerce introduced new contractual relationships. Communications made for greater mobility. The pace of social change quickened. The colonial powers introduced French, Portuguese, British, and Belgian legal systems. In accordance with their respective policies, they tried to provide for heterogeneous groups with widely differing mores and for individuals of different cultures and standards of living—in short, for the plural societies that emerged. In some instances (in Northern Nigeria and Senegal, for example, where the existence of Islamic law added to an already difficult situation), the variety of religions provided additional complicating factors.

The colonial powers dealt with the situation differently. The Portuguese made no provision for indigenous law and custom. Though the Belgians and the French took note of it, they adopted policies that assumed that Africans must adapt themselves increasingly to their European systems of law—Africans must, they postulated, move up the ladder of civilization to the acceptance of European laws. The British recognized indigenous customs and institutions, and accordingly, they legalized and instituted, side by side, two sets of laws and procedures. Each system of the colonial powers has left its legacy of problems.

Laws must be a part of a society's norms of behavior and must reflect its experience, its values, and its goals. Each new African nation is faced with the problem of legal pluralism. In each new African nation, peoples of different traditions have come under a common rule, and a legal system must be devised to fit the new situation.

Despite their respective problems, all the African countries that came under colonial rule had to deal with certain common aspects of the impact of European law. European legal concepts and, along with them, procedures were imposed on all of these countries. Community life, once regulated by customary laws, which were expected to be understood by all adults, was now subject to laws imposed by an alien ruler. The procedures were such as only the initiate could know; they were not only extraneous but also baffling. As it became more and more familiar, and once-accepted practices were decreed to be punishable offenses, the new legal system became something obeyed not because it reflected the community's experience or desires, but because it represented the will of the ruler.

The mystification of law, and its divorce from the active daily life of the community, made the legal profession a necessary and lucrative one in Africa. Litigants needed guidance through the maze that the law became to the majority of citizens. This situation has had the effect of altering the essential nature of law as a social institution reflecting societal norms and goals. It is a situation that calls out to be rectified.

The impact of European law has had not only legal but political consequences. European law, particularly that of the French and that of the British, carried with it ideas that were bound sooner or later to prove explosive. These concepts rested implicitly, and sometimes explicitly, on doctrines of natural rights, rationalism, and individualism, concepts that could bear universal application. In due course the inferences were drawn.

In the French territories, for example, the notion of two different classes of citizens, subject to two different systems of law and procedure, was contrary to the basic assumptions of France's own legal system. The preamble to the historic French Declaration of the Rights of Man and of the Citizen *(Déclaration des droits de l'homme et du citoyen)* read:

The representatives of the French people, constituted in a national assembly, considering that ignorance, oblivion, or contempt of the rights of man are the only causes of public misfortunes and of the corruption of governments, have resolved to lay down, in a solemn declaration, the natural, inalienable and sacred rights of man, in order that this declaration, being always before all members of the social body, should constantly remind them of their rights and their duties; that the actions of the legislative as well as of the executive power, being liable at any moment to be referred to the end of all political institutions, should be more respected; that the grievances of the citizen, being henceforward based upon simple and indisputable principles, should always be conducive to the preservation of the Constitution and to the happiness of all.

It may well be that on August 26, 1789, the French National Assembly that adopted the Declaration had only Frenchmen in mind, but its effect has been wider. Though many of the French subjects of Africa could not read these words when colonization began, the time came when they could read, and infer, and claim that the "natural . . . rights of man" and the "simple and indisputable principles" should indeed "always be conducive to the . . . happiness of all," and that "man" included not only white men, not only a favored few persons who were admitted to the status of first-class citizens, but all men. The slogan of the French Revolution, "Liberty, Equality, Fraternity," must apply to all mankind.

The same ideas were inherent in British law and tradition. They were given explicit and memorable expression in the American Declaration of Independence of 1776, the underlying assumptions of which were those of British law. John Locke is recalled in the American Declaration:

We hold these truths to be self-evident, that all men are created equal, that they are endowed by their Creator with certain unalienable Rights, that among these are Life, Liberty and the pursuit of Happiness. That to secure these rights,

Governments are instituted among Men, deriving their just powers from the consent of the governed. That whenever any Form of Government becomes destructive of these ends, it is the Right of the People to alter or to abolish it, and to institute new Government, laying its foundation on such principles and organizing its powers in such form, as to them shall seem most likely to effect their Safety and Happiness.

The impact of such concepts was bound to be revolutionary. Even in the colonies, British law accorded personal freedom to the subject. Equality before the law could not be long divorced from racial equality, and this in turn struck at the very root of colonialism. There can be no justification for treating the African as a second-class citizen in the face of such accepted pronouncements. So colonialism has bred nationalism as a reaction to the practices and assumptions of European administration and law. Africans demand acceptance as equals, for "all men are created equal," and are "endowed . . . with certain unalienable Rights," among them, the right of a people to freedom from colonial domination.

But there has always been a wide gap between professed ideals and actual practice, and so there have been bitter wars in the struggle for independence from colonial powers. This struggle, which began in the British North American colonies, continues its tragic drama in French Algeria and Portuguese Angola. The last act is yet to come.

6. The Challenge of Education

THERE is a close link between African education and African nationalism. Europe brought to Africa a heritage of education carried on through formal schooling. In the schools that missionaries and European governments established in Africa, Africans were given the key to new knowledge. They learned to read and write and to absorb new ideas—ideas, such as those quoted in the previous chapter, of natural rights, human dignity, and equality.

In Africa, as elsewhere, education is a potent instrument of social change. It has imparted new skills, which aided Africa's economic development. And it has also fostered the emergence of a new class of Africans—a class of literate people. This was bound to affect social relations among the citizens of a colony, where the achievement of new roles, and increased status, became possible, and also between the educated Africans and their European mentors. Education is the vehicle of ideas, and in the words of the English philosopher G. Lowes Dickensen, "whatever men may say or think, ideas are the greatest force in the world."

African communities did have their own forms of education. Every community had its ways of passing on to the next generation its own culture, its own way of life. This is education in its broad social context—what the French sociologist Émile Durkheim defined as "the action exercised by the generations of adults on those who are not yet ready for social life."

⟨In most African communities, those who were not yet ready for social life were prepared for it through day-by-day association of the young with the old. Training for special roles was accomplished through informal instruction given by persons already filling those roles, often members of one's own family or kingroup. In other matters, every adult was an instructor of the young. (In many an African village, an adult passerby may still be seen correcting some wrong behavior of the young or explaining some ongoing activity of adults.) Societies were small and stable enough for these informal methods to suffice. The cultural heritage, as much of it as was necessary for adult life, could be learned in this way, through informal instruction and participation.⟩

That situation has changed. There has been the invasion of European technology, and of European administration. Societies have become larger and more heterogeneous. There are more ways of earning a living, and there has been increasing specialization. It is no longer possible to train the young adequately for social life through the traditional informal methods.

Everywhere in Africa, even illiterate adults eagerly seek schooling for their children, and are prepared to make big personal sacrifices to secure it for them. Formal schooling has now come to be regarded as essential not only for equipping the individual to earn a living but also for equipping Africa's peoples for nationhood. The formal education introduced by Europeans has come to be accepted as an indispensable lever for progress in all aspects of life. Schooling is, in fact, increasingly becoming a part of African culture, a borrowed institution fitting into the pattern of living.

Some parts of Africa inherited a tradition of reading and writing long before the period of European colonization; it came to them from the Arab world, through the Islamic religion. But to the majority of countries in Africa, reading and writing came from Europe. It was European missionaries who pioneered education in Africa, and from the sixteenth century to the present day, Christian missions of different churches have played a prominent role in the education of the African. Through this, the impact of Christianity on Africa has been greater than the number of converts to Christianity would indicate.

The fact that formal education was first introduced by the churches affected its character. It was both Christian and European in orientation. But under the auspices of the respective governments of the African territories, the educational systems also reflected the policies of the colonizing powers. These policies have come in for criticism because of their postulates and failures.

The earliest European schools in Africa were established in the Portuguese African colony of Angola, when the first Catholic mission opened there, in 1534. Despite this early start, the indigenous populations in Portuguese African colonies have illiteracy rates that are among the highest in the world; about 95 per cent of the African populations of Angola and Mozambique are illiterate. The Roman Catholic mission has carried out most of the educational work that has been done, acting as an agent of the state. In accordance with state policy, the Catholic Church has been, in the words of the Colonial Act of 1930, "an instrument of civilization and national influence." Portuguese policy has been to use the schools as vehicles to spread the Portuguese language and culture. Africans who sufficiently assimilate it move up the social ladder to join the class of *assimilado,* the class of those who are counted with the *civilizada* section of the population, to which the Europeans belong. The majority of the Africans are not *civilizada* and cannot be, for Portugal's policy is clearly designed to discourage African advance. There is no indication of any conception of independence or responsibility for the Africans, and accordingly, the educational policy offers little opportunity for progress.

In Spanish territories, the official aim of education for Africans is to encourage "the spread of patriotism and the Spanish virtues and culture, without uprooting the African, but with the definite purpose of improving his living conditions." * It is a policy that sets no higher goal for the educated African than that he should be an "auxiliary"—as a teacher, or in commercial, health, or other public service, or as an agricultural worker. There is no vision of the African other than in some position subordinate to that of the European.

The Belgians did far more than the Portuguese or the Spaniards in the way of education for their colonial subjects in Africa. But they, too, had narrow vision, and accordingly, their policy seems to have been limited to training Africans for manual, clerical and minor technical jobs only. The avowed aim, as put by L. Franck, Minister of the Colonies in 1920, was "to produce better Africans, and not Europeans who could never be more than humans of a third category." The utilitarian outlook caused excessive emphasis to be laid on vocational training. Through the agency of the Catholic Church, which was entrusted with education, a creditable amount of work was done on African languages and in manual, vocational, and technical training, but little was done to prepare the African population for independence and the responsibility that independence entailed. The pace was too leisurely and slow. When the "wind of change" compelled the Belgian Govern-

---

* Lord Hailey, *An African Survey* (rev. ed.; London and New York: Oxford University Press, 1956), p. 1220.

ment to concede a hurried independence to the Congo, the shortcomings of Belgium's educational policy became obvious. It seemed that its sole purpose had been to produce useful citizens providing labor in the economic cooperation between African resources and Belgian capital, Belgian knowledge, and Belgian skills. It was not conceived that Africans should aspire to the higher levels of the social hierarchy.

African subjects of French and British colonies were given more opportunity, and consequently, they made greater advances. The policies of the two countries were, however, different. France had a consistent policy, but Britain, to all appearances, did not.

As early as 1816, the French Government opened a school in Saint-Louis, Senegal, where an attempt was made to teach the Senegalese through the medium of their own Wolof language. The experiment was not successful, and French policy changed. The emphasis shifted to the teaching of French language and culture. The aim became one of training an African elite, which would be French in outlook, at home in French culture, and able to assist in the task of administering the overseas territories. Accordingly, the schools and colleges of the French overseas territories became vehicles for spreading French culture. The whole trend was to produce a civilization that was essentially French, "conceived and organized in the ideological context of assimilation," as one observer has put it. As for the mass of the population, it was to receive an education that would enable its members to become good farmers in the rural areas, or wage earners in the towns. For a long time, these were the objectives of French educational policy. After World War II, the status of citizenship was extended to more Africans. This was followed by the granting of independence to the overseas territories. These developments made it clear that the concept of one type of education for an elite and another for the mass of the population was a wrong one. Nevertheless, the policy did succeed in forging firm links between France and its overseas territories. The relationship between the French and the African elite has been remarkable for its absence of color prejudice and bitterness, and for the successful achievement of the objective of "association." But it does not fulfill the aspirations of independent territories eager to express their own identity through their own cultures.

In the British colonies, missionary activity and local response, rather than official policy (which was neither clear nor uniform), dictated the character and pace of education. The colonial governments gave financial assistance and, through their education departments, supervision, which encouraged and protected good standards. Missionary influence, the examinations system, and British experience made the education generally Christian and British in orientation, but each colony established its own schools and colleges without being restrained by any fixed policy of the British Government.

Turning to the educational policy of the Republic of South Africa, one recalls what Cicero wrote long ago: "Men differ in knowledge, but are equal in ability to learn; there is no race that, guided by reason, cannot obtain virtue." The Republic has adopted a policy by which education is to be used, not to provide a bridge between Europeans and Africans, but to keep them apart. The Education Act of 1953 defined the policy as one that would "prepare the natives more effectively for their future occupations." These occupations are to be subordinate positions; for, despite the avowed aim of enabling each section to develop in the context of its own culture, the Union's objective is clearly to perpetuate European domination. In the words of a report published by the Methodist Church Conference of 1954, the Education Act aimed "at conditioning the African people to be in a permanent position of subordination to the State," and in the South African context, the state means the European section of the community, for the Europeans are the rulers.

In the pursuit of these various policies, primary, secondary, technical, and vocational schools, teacher-training colleges, and universities have been built. These facilities have been inherited by African governments in the territories that are now independent. In view of the contributions education is expected to make to nation building and development, past policies and achievements have been subjected to criticism and reappraisal.

A general criticism is that the colonial powers failed to accord education the high priority it deserved. Too few people have been educated for the many tasks that now required literate Africans. This is supported by the facts. The UNESCO report on *World Illiteracy at Mid-Century* showed the illiteracy rates for Africa as ranging from 45 to 50 per cent in Basutoland to over 95 per cent in Angola, Mozambique, and the Somalilands. The median for the whole continent lay between 85 and 90 per cent. The average illiteracy rate for the whole world was estimated at 43 to 45 per cent. Thus, in 1950, most African countries had strikingly higher illiteracy rates than were to be found elsewhere in the world.

It is estimated that 100 million adults in Africa cannot read or write. With regard to children of school age, available figures from UNESCO's *Manual of Education Statistics, 1961* show that, in the majority of African countries, more than 80 per cent of these children (five to nineteen years old) are not enrolled in school. The ratio of pupil enrollment to school-age population ranges from under 2 per cent in the Niger Republic and the former British Somaliland to nearly 60 per cent in Western Nigeria and Southern Rhodesia; the median for the continent is around 16 per cent. If only the ratio of enrollment in primary schools to the primary-school-age (five to fourteen years) population is considered, the range is from under 3 per cent in the former British Somaliland to nearly 100 per cent in Western Nigeria, and the median for the continent is around 25 per cent. But the figures for individual countries show that, in the majority of African countries, 60 per cent of the children of primary-school age are not attending school; in some areas (former British Somaliland, the Niger Republic, Ethiopia, Upper Volta, Mauritania, Mali, and Northern Nigeria, for example) 90 per cent or more of the primary-school-age children are not enrolled in school.

The statistics of secondary-school enrollments in the different countries are not easy to compare—conditions vary too much—but the general picture for Africa is one of insufficient educational facilities at all levels, from primary school to university. In 1960, facilities for higher education were available in only nineteen African states, and the total enrollment in all of them was 120,000. Slightly more than 90 per cent of this enrollment was in higher institutions in North Africa, in Morocco, Algeria, Tunisia, Libya, and Egypt; only 11,500 students were enrolled in the other territories. This does not give the complete picture of Africans receiving higher education, for at least 12,000 were studying in higher institutions in Europe and America; but it does show the paucity of available facilities within Africa.

In about two-thirds of the countries in Africa, the annual investment in education is less than five dollars per head. In several countries, it is less than one dollar per head. Looked at in another way, the amount allocated to education in many countries in Africa is less than 3 per cent of national income.

The general awareness of this situation is shown by the fact that whenever any African country has become independent, one of the first steps the new rulers have taken is to increase educational facilities. This is sufficient commentary on the previous policies and achievements of the colonial powers with regard to education. Though, in many cases, formal schooling was introduced by nationals of these powers, the colonial conception of education's role in the development of Africa was unimaginative, and consequently, as subsequent events have shown, in no instance, not even in the British and French territories, were adequate educational provisions made. Education did not have a high enough priority.

Criticism has also been leveled at the content of education in Africa. Are the schools teaching the right things? Or has African education been too bookish and narrow, and insufficiently related to the cultural backgrounds and the needs and aspirations of African societies?

Education has been oriented—in some cases, as a matter of deliberate policy—to the societies and cultures of the colonial powers. What should be taught? And how should it be taught? These are challenging questions as far as Africa is concerned.

Many of those who go to school in Africa end their formal schooling at the primary level—that is, after six to ten years (the period varies in the different countries) of schooling. Then they are launched into life, and where illiteracy rates are so high, often into positions of responsibility. What account should be taken of this in designing school courses of study? Should the primary school be regarded only as a preparation for secondary school when it is known that only a small proportion of those who go through the primary schools have the opportunity to attend secondary schools? Similar questions are raised about secondary schools.

It would be unrealistic in the context of Africa to treat the secondary school as if it were merely a preparation for university education. It is true that education at each level depends on that at the level above, which, in turn, is dependent on it. In Africa this raises special problems. One of them (to which attention has been drawn in investigations recently carried out on the structure of educational institutions in such African countries as Nigeria) is the obvious imbalance between the successive levels of the educational ladder—between primary and secondary schools and between secondary schools and institutions of higher education. Where should the emphasis be? How should a country expand educational facilities and, at the same time, avoid short-term oversupplies of primary- or secondary-school leavers?

Many countries, especially in West Africa, are faced with unemployment among primary-school leavers because there has been too rapid an expansion of primary schools without coordination with other levels or with the manpower needs of the societies. This has led to new insights into educational planning. Educational planning is now considered within the framework of over-all development with which it should be coordinated, a framework that includes, for example, the manpower needs of the country. The costing of educational development within this context requires cooperation between educators and economists.

The question of what shall be taught is also bound up with the desire that education in the schools should take account of African society and culture. As a corollary to this, new textbooks are needed. In the context of the needs of the society, there is also much criticism of the neglect of agriculture, from which the majority of the peoples of Africa earn their living. There are complaints of the lack of young people sufficiently trained or willing to engage in agricultural work.

There is a need to examine and improve not only curriculums but also teaching methods. One question concerns the use being made of new media of communication, not only for teaching in the schools, but also for tackling what is an acute problem for Africa—the battle against illiteracy. One of these media is radio. It is estimated that there are about 365 million radio receivers in use around the world. Only 4.5 million, or less than 1.3 per cent, are found in the whole of Africa; this works out to fewer than 20 radios per 1,000 inhabitants. In the Niger, Rwanda, Burundi, Upper Volta, Sudan, and Mauritania, there is not even 1 radio per 1,000 inhabitants. The best-supplied areas, where there are more than 50 radios per 1,000 inhabitants, are Egypt, the Republic of South Africa, and French Somaliland. Another medium is the cinema. The available data show that there are 5 cinema seats per 1,000 inhabitants in Africa, and the average attendance at commercial cinemas is only once a year per inhabitant. These modern media of communication, which could be effective vehicles of education, are not available to millions of Africans.

The effectiveness of curriculums and teaching methods and media of communication must depend on teachers. Everywhere in Africa there is a shortage not only of teachers but also of colleges for training them.

Another special problem, revealed in all education statistics for Africa, is the disparity between the number of boys and the number of girls at school. This inequality has indicated that girls' education should receive special attention.

Many who are anxious to see rapid economic and technical development in Africa find that the weakest link in the educational systems inherited from colonial powers is the lack of technicians at all levels. Technicians are not only in short supply, but the facilities for training them are very inadequate.

In short, the problem of education in Africa is not merely one of extending facilities, but also of examining the whole process of education to see how it can be used in the context of modernization and nation building. African countries have increasingly come to regard education as a potent tool for economic and social development; accordingly, they have given it high priority in development plans. At a UNESCO Conference of African States held in 1961 on the Development of Education in Africa, after a realistic and comprehensive review of the situation, the participants agreed on and emphasized the point that education is a factor in the economic growth of a country and therefore a gainful economic investment. This endorses a view of education which has already inspired the plans and policies of a number of independent African countries, such as Senegal, Ghana, and Nigeria. But viewed against the policies of colonial powers, it represents a new outlook, for education has previously been regarded only as an item of consumption. The new concept is reflected in increasing educational expenditures by all independent African territories, and in acceptance of the view that education may be properly financed even from loans.

The tasks expected of education are many. There is need for supplementing the supply of manpower at all levels; for eliminating illiteracy; and for preparing the adult population for the responsibilities of modern citizenship. There are not only problems of quantity, but problems of quality too.

As the survey of the educational policies of the colonizing powers has made evident, education in many parts of Africa was directed toward goals set by the metropolitan countries and reflected their social experience and needs rather than those of Africa. In the former French colonies, for example, the curriculums and content of secondary schools and higher institutions still conform to those of France; and in the former British colonies, examination requirements still make it necessary to follow the British system. In both cases, one reason for the continued adherence to the old is the desire to maintain high standards.

As noted above, the problem is how to reform education so as to ensure that the schools and colleges are rooted in African soil and life and, at the same time, meet the needs for economic and social advance. For this reason, Africans, and others, have raised questions about the content of education—how much general education should be provided? how much specialization should there be? at what level should it begin? what place should African studies have in the educational system?—as well as about such related problems as the connections between the arts and the sciences. Much thinking is going on, and much research and views are being exchanged at international conferences.

In view of the stress on African culture that African nationalism now demands, it may well be asked if there is anything in African traditional methods of education that is of value, or of relevance, to contemporary issues. There is one thing. And it is an important one at that. In the traditional systems of education in Africa, there was not much knowledge of science to impart, and the tribal communities did not have to cope with complex questions of the balance between primary and secondary schools, secondary schools and colleges, or with the riddles of the costing of education. No guidance is offered from Africa's own past for these matters. But it is noteworthy that in the traditional forms of education, there was much emphasis on behavior, on good and evil as the society saw it, in terms of its own survival and continuity. Education was for life, for the fulfillment of social obligations. It was rooted in the person, and in his behavior. This was essentially right. Education must be concerned with what human beings become. The need for technicians and productive skills must not be allowed to obscure this. Of all Africa's resources, her young people are the most valuable. Educators and planners have a responsibility to consider what sort of human beings come out of the educational institutions they plan; for in the last resort, it is this that will determine the quality of life, and the role that Africa plays in the world.

There is a social situation in Africa that should influence educational planning. The rapid social changes going on, the upheavals, the conflict in standards and values, the increase of acquisitiveness and of crime, all make it of compelling importance that thinking and research about education be guided by the fact that education is primarily concerned with what sort of persons people become. Skilled men and women, technicians, scientists, and the like are all needed. There must be industrialization if standards of living are to go up appreciably. But training, even for the narrow objective of industrialization, cannot be successful if education is solely in utilitarian terms; for industrial life, like any other, demands standards of discipline and responsibility, attitudes and behavior, without which it cannot function properly. The quality of life counts.

Age does not change what is true, for truth has an everlasting youth. The ancient Greek scholars gave much thought to education and wrote some very profound things about its purposes. Among those that are worth recalling are the words of Plato, who wrote:

> It is not the life of knowledge, not even if it included all the sciences, that creates happiness and well-being, but a single branch of knowledge—the science of good and evil. If you exclude this from other branches, medicine will be equally able to give us health, and shoemaking shoes, and weaving clothes. But without the knowledge of good and evil, the use and excellence of these sciences will be found to fail us.

We are frequently told nowadays that the peace of the world, indeed human life itself, is in danger because men have acquired more power from science and technology than they have the morality to use. Many would endorse what Plato taught: "The noblest of all studies is the study of what men should be and how they should live." This was always what, according to their lights, African tribes were concerned with in their informal methods of education. Social virtues were taught to the young through social life. It was an education concerned with what the young became as adults and with what they did as members of society—with the fulfillment of their social obligations.

The challenge of education offered to and by the emergent states of Africa is a challenge to think afresh, within the context of our contemporary life and the opportunities offered by contemporary science and technology, about what education can do to foster an international community based on men and women who have been adequately prepared not only to be good men and women but also to be good citizens of a world that consists of many nations, all of which share in mutual sympathy and respect, in a common humanity.

III

*THE CHALLENGE
OF COMMON HUMANITY
AND MORALITY*

7. *This Dark Skin*

THE last chapter closed with the words "all of which share in mutual sympathy and respect, in a common humanity."

Race relations in Africa constitute an acute international problem. Behind the various policies we have encountered lies the common element of relations between Europeans and Africans, between white and black people. At best, the policies have been marked by liberal paternalism; at worst, by unyielding white ascendancy.

There is a passage in Shakespeare *(Love's Labour's Lost,* Act IV, Sc. 3) which is germane to the subject of this chapter:

> Black is the badge of hell,
> The hue of dungeons and the scowl of night.

Black seems to be connected with what is evil, or feared; and men tend to be savage toward the objects of their fear.

Slavery is a very old institution. Whites have enslaved whites. And blacks have enslaved blacks. But in the long period of the slave trade, from the sixteenth century until the trade was abolished in the nineteenth, millions of black men and women were taken from Africa to be enslaved to whites. What is common to all slavery is that one man treats another as his property; but when a black man becomes the slave of a white man, added to the difference in status between slave and master is the difference in color between black and white. The dark-skinned man becomes the subordinate of the pale-skinned man, and black becomes the "badge of hell," of all that is dark, inferior, and contemptible.

About 97 per cent of the 280 million inhabitants of the continent of Africa are of African descent and have dark skins. Of the remainder, approximately 6 million are of European origin, and 800,000 are Pakistanis and Indians, who are also colored people. Half of the whites live in the Republic of South Africa; a third live in North Africa; the rest are scattered unevenly over the continent, with substantial concentrations in Southern Rhodesia, Angola, Kenya, Northern Rhodesia, and, until recently, the Congo. All of these areas with substantial concentrations of whites are actual or potential seats of racial turmoil.

The fact that blacks have been slaves to whites has never been forgotten. On top of slavery, came the colonization of Africa and the subjection of its blacks to European rule. This, again, was a domination of blacks by whites, and one in which, as we have observed, political and social policies were based on the premise that blacks are inferior to whites.

To justify colonialism, efforts have been made to find scientific theories to establish the supposed innate inferiority of the African. We have encountered the biological theory of the survival of the fitter race, a theory in which the conquest of Africans in war was cited as evidence attesting to their inferiority. Measurements of the black man's head and studies of skeletons and craniums were invoked, with all their long and learned-sounding terminology (dolichocephalic and all that), in efforts to prove that the African belonged to a lower species than the European; but he was too much of a man to be an ape. The evidence that he

belonged to the one species of man—Homo sapiens—was
too overwhelming to be toppled. *9 7/15*

Still, it was felt there must be some fundamental difference. It was sought in the "primitive" culture of the African.
Anthropologists found that his religion was full of fear—
fear of spirits, ghosts, demons, witches; fear of misfortunes
that will be inflicted by vengeful spirits and gods. There
were also the bizarre rituals. But later anthropologists, with
better empirical methods of research, convincingly showed
that some of the earlier writings were based on incorrect or
insufficient data—and that there were respectable and intelligible elements in the beliefs, worship, and rituals of African peoples. Even so, some anthropologists persisted in
treating the African as, at best, a child; he could not be
treated as an adult; he could not be as mature as the white
man. So there was developed the image of tribal innocence
—the simple African living in idyllic simplicity in his native
bower. But others discovered too much savagery in the African to accept this picture of innocent simplicity. They
directed attention to tribal feuds, to reports of cannibalism
in certain regions, ritual murders in others; surely, these
were the marks of savagery. The intellect of the African must
be different from that of the white man. Learned disserta-
tions appeared on the mind of the primitive, savage African.
It was alleged that his intelligence quotient was low; his
vocabulary had no abstract nouns; he was incapable of
abstract thinking; he had no philosophy; he did not understand natural phenomena. Nature was a universe peopled
by him with spirits. He had no idea of causality. His mind
was full of magical notions. This stereotype is still alive.
As recently as 1953, General Norton de Matos, former
Governor of the Portuguese territory of Angola, could write:

In Africa our objective has been to convert the blacks, to lift
them from the moral and material misery they were in when

we encountered them, to clothe them, to give them human habitation, to make them rural proprietors, or to transform them into artisans.*

But there were other aspects of African cultures, and these did not fit into the picture. Complex social organizations, group loyalties, African music, rhythms, and art, the African's capacity to learn just as quickly and easily as any other human being—none of these fit the image. So another deficiency was fastened upon—the African's tools were inefficient; his technology was backward. But further archaeological and anthropological studies revealed ancient cities and civilizations, and chiefdoms famed for their grandeur; and there were well-organized contemporary kingdoms too, with political structures and cultures that commanded respect. Attention was then focused on another obvious lack—Africa had no tradition of writing. Studies began to appear on the nonliterate societies. And so, over the years, evidence has been built up to show that the cultures of African peoples are inferior to those of whites; and this must be because Africans belong to an inferior race.

If the problem of race relations between white and black really depended on scientific or intellectual proof, there would be some point in taking a look at some of these theories and findings. But that has been done in many books. There have been works by anthropologists, archaeologists, sociologists—scientists of all races—controverting and disproving some of the many theories, opinions, and misconceptions about Africans. So far no success has attended the efforts of those anthropologists and archaeologists who have tried to link cultures with race. No correlation between cultures and genetic qualities of racial types has been irrefutably established.

Cultures are learned, and, as the social changes going on

* *Africa Nossa*, 1953, p. 15.

in Africa attest, cultures change. Religious beliefs and practices change. There are converts to Christianity and to Islam in Africa. Social institutions change. There are trade unions and parliamentary institutions in Africa today. New techniques are being learned. Industrialization has begun. Illiteracy rates are high, but there is a growing body of literate Africans; schools, colleges, and universities are increasing in number. All of this is taking place without any changes in the biological or genetic constitution of African peoples. There are indeed aspects of traditional cultures, including religious beliefs and practices, which must change if they are to take account of new knowledge, new social situations. But no support for the innate inferiority of the African can be found in this; all human cultures and institutions undergo change.

UNESCO assembled a body of internationally respected scientists and scholars—anthropologists, archaeologists, and sociologists—to study the question of race. In 1953, this group issued an authoritative statement to the effect that no scientific basis could be found for the belief that one race was inferior or superior to another. In a subsequent UNESCO publication on *Race and Culture,* Mr. Michel Lieris, an eminent anthropologist, had this to say: "It is fruitless to seek in the biology of race an explanation of the difference observable between the cultural achievements of the various peoples."* He cited examples to show that cultural development is not uniform, even within a single country; for "the music, painting, and sculpture or architecture of some country will pass through a brilliant period and then for some centuries at least nothing further of note will be produced." Mr. Lieris then went on to point out that the cultural achievements of any country represent the combined efforts of many peoples. With respect to the contemporary position of Europe, he wrote: "The peoples of Europe—whose over-

* *Race and Culture* (Paris: UNESCO, 1958), p. 33.

seas expansion, be it remembered, is of very recent date, today restricted by the evolution of the very peoples they formerly surpassed in techniques—owed their cultural lead to the opportunities they have long had of frequent contacts among themselves and with contrasting peoples. . . . The truth is all cultures have their successes and failures, their faults and virtues."*

In another UNESCO publication, *Race and History*,† Mr. Claude Lewi-Strauss advances arguments and cites many examples to show that " 'cumulative' history is not the prerogative of any one civilization or period." He agrees with Mr. Lieris, for he, too, makes the point that the culture of any one country at any given time is the result of countless interactions, countless interchanges of ideas, and the cumulative experience of generations.

The truth is that, on the subject of race relations, particularly as between black and white, it is not what science has to say that matters. Race attitudes are not determined by the validity, or lack of validity, of scientific data. Men did not stop to find a causal relation between cultural phenomena and biological or genetic data before they embarked on slavery or colonization or segregation. The race attitudes were arrived at before proper consideration of the facts. They are prejudices.

John Masefield, the Poet Laureate of England, has a delightful poem called "Laugh and Be Merry," in which appear the lines:

> Laugh and be merry together, like brothers akin,
> Guesting awhile in the rooms of a beautiful inn.

The majority of white people do not wish to accept the blacks "like brothers akin," and so the "inn" is nearer to being chaotic than beautiful.

* *Ibid.*, p. 34.
† Paris: UNESCO, 1958.

Fortunately, there are a few white people who do accept the blacks as "brothers akin." There would be no hope for mankind otherwise. Some of those who do have gone out to Africa over the years—as missionaries, teachers, doctors, nurses, scholars, civil servants, and businessmen—and have given their sincere, devoted service to Africa. This indeed must be acknowledged. Were African nationalists to become too bitter to recognize it, they would be blocking the entrance to the only hopeful avenue open to men seeking international harmony and peace; for happy race relations can be achieved only when mutual sympathy and respect are given expression in service to others, sincerely offered, gratefully accepted, and when possible, reciprocated. Whites and blacks must work together to make harmonious human relations possible. It is more a matter of the heart than of genetics. Happy race relations can no more be built on a rankling sense of grievance than on an arrogant sense of superiority.

Slavery, colonial subjection, the color bar, second-class citizenship, segregation, discrimination, apartheid—that is the black man's lot. It is a sad lot, apportioned by the white man. What does the African think of it all?

The Akan peoples of Ghana have an aphorism that gives the answer. The saying evidently derived from their experience of farming, the main source of livelihood. When a farmer makes a new farm, he clears a plot in the middle of a forest. The cleared plot is surrounded by a wilderness of tall trees and thick undergrowth. Where the cultivated plot touches the uncultivated is the *nhanoa,* the edge of cultivation, the boundary. Pregnantly, the Akan people say: *Honam mu nni nhanao.* (In human flesh there is no edge of cultivation—no boundary.) It is the Akan way of saying that all human flesh is of one kind; all mankind is one species.

An Akan child is taught to greet all whom he meets; even the stranger whom he may never meet again. It is more than courtesy. The greeting is considered to be an acknowledgement, a recognition of the other person as a fellow human being. If you passed him by without greeting him, you would be treating him as a thing—you would be implying that he did not share your humanity. We have noted that a high value was placed on human relations in traditional African societies. To recognize one whom you passed as a fellow human being was an obligation.

An Akan person is deeply hurt when he is given cause to say, "He behaved toward me as though I were not a human being." In this instance, the Akan may speak for all Africans. This is the heart of the matter. It is a question of the basic equality of mankind, of the membership of men, all men, in just one species.

Much has been done—and much is still being done— in Africa, America, and elsewhere by the pale-skinned man against the dark-skinned man. Slavery, colonial rule, segregation, discrimination, apartheid—it is not the illegality, not the injustice, that rouses the deepest sense of grievance. It is the degradation the treatment implies or is interpreted to imply. It is the fact that one man can say truthfully that another "behaved toward me as though I were not a human being." All the technical theories, all the analyses of culture and race, all the attempts to establish the innate inferiority of the African are vain efforts. They get away from the fact. The dark skin clothes a human being in every whit as human as the pale. This is the challenge of common humanity. It is taking a long, long time for the white man, in America, in Europe, or in Africa, to accept it. Progress has been made, but it has been slow—dangerously slow for the peace and harmony of mankind.

Just as there are whites who see the problem in this light, and who have shown by their behavior that they accept the dark-skinned person as a brother, so there are many Africans who, despite the wrongs they or their peoples have suffered, despite the degradation, are able to "Laugh and be proud to belong to the old proud pageant of man."

The late Dr. Kwegyir Aggrey, a great African whose life was devoted to working and living for the brotherhood of man and for cooperation between black and white, left us the beautiful imagery of the black and white keys of a piano; you can, he taught, make some sort of music on the white keys of the piano alone, or on the black keys alone, but for real harmony, you need both the white and the black keys. He believed that harmonious relations between black and white could be achieved, and he held to this belief in spite of humiliating experiences in the deep South of the United States and in the Union of South Africa. His optimism was rooted in his faith in Christ. As a sincere and devoted Christian, he was able to say: "To those who have might, I want to give a might mightier than man's. I want to sing a song of hope to the despairing; to breathe the breath of love that will chase away all hating. I believe that right will ultimately conquer wrong, virtue conquer vice, harmony take the place of discords." His biographer called him "Aggrey of Africa," and so he has been accepted by all; for, because he was a good man, he was one of those who belong to all men and to all ages.

Segregation, apartheid, and discrimination seem to be based on the conviction that race and culture permanently divide Europeans and Africans; that, as Kipling wrote:

> East is East, and West is West,
> And never the twain shall meet.

To this, the late Indian poet Rabindranath Tagore gave an impressive reply: "The twain shall meet in amity, peace, and mutual understanding, and this will lead to a holy wedlock before the common altar of humanity."

The dark skin is Africa's biggest challenge to the world,

and especially to the white man, who at this particular point of history has superior technological power.

The starting point of harmonious race relations is the recognition that each race is like the other—that all men are equal in their humanity.

8. The Challenge of Morality

In discussing relations between Europe and Africa, especially with the Algerian war just ended and Angola still in ferment, it would seem more realistic to write about nuclear tests in the Sahara or economic blockades against Portugal. To write about common humanity and mutual sympathy and respect with reference to relations between Africans and Europeans is to display one's naïveté.

Sentiments like John Greenleaf Whittier's should belong to the dreamy world of Sunday church services and not to the stark and real world of white-black relations:

> Then shall all shackles fall; the stormy clangour
> Of wild war-music o'er the earth shall cease;
> Love shall tread out the baleful fire of anger,
> And in its ashes plant the tree of peace.

Yet it is precisely into this forbidden realm of morality that we venture in this short chapter—in the conviction that relations between Europeans and Africans, as indeed all human relations, belong to the realm of morals. Human relationships must have moral foundations; they cannot be built on anything else. The challenge that segregation, discrimination, apartheid, and colonialism pose is essentially a moral one.

Europe has technological power. New technological achievements—the invasion of outer space, the placing of men into orbit around the earth—all point to new dangers as well as to new opportunities for mankind. It is now hackneyed to note that these new dangers threaten mankind with annihilation. The nations that can afford it are spending vast amounts of money in efforts to ensure peace by piling up nuclear and other powerful weapons of destruction. The small and poor states of Africa cannot enter the arms race. The task of developing human and natural resources to make life a little more tolerable for the majority of citizens is formidable enough.

But Africa has an interest in world peace; it is a necessary condition for even the smallest modicum of development. Africa's contribution need not be along the path of piling up arms, but it could be in the moral sphere. African traditional cultures may not have much to offer the highly technological modern world. But there is, in all of them, something that is relevant to white and black relationships and to the present world situation.

We return to the common characteristic of traditional African cultures—the important role that kinship plays. Love and service are taught through the kingroup, which is the basis of social and political life. Man, and the social relations of men, come first; the things to serve the needs of men come second. This is the quintessence of African traditional cultures. Now, as the new states of Africa are entering the international scene, this heritage from their own past should be used to make a major contribution to world peace. It should remind the world that the true path to harmonious relations lies in focusing attention on human beings and in accepting obligations and responsibility in a spirit of brotherhood among human beings.

The two universal religions that have converts in Africa are Christianity and Islam, both of which agree on the doctrine of the brotherhood of man. That doctrine inculcates the moral rule that one should act toward others as one would have others act toward oneself. Its acceptance involves one with one's neighbors in obligations that demand many and sometimes costly practical works.

At a conference that the Congress for Cultural Freedom held in Milan in the summer of 1955, one of the participants, an ex-cabinet minister of Britain, said during a discussion of the problems of economic development and freedom in underdeveloped countries: "The Western nations have a moral duty to help the underdeveloped countries substantially, just as within each nation most of us now agree that there is a moral duty to tax the rich to help the poor." That was before the idea of aid to the underdeveloped countries had become as acceptable to governments as it is today. This general acceptance is a remarkable evidence of moral advance; for, basically, the idea that citizens of the industrial countries should be taxed in order that aid may be given to the poorer countries can only be justified on moral grounds. It is the application of the golden rule in the international sphere.

Positive contributions toward easing the race tensions of Africa—and, indeed, international tensions as well—can be made through activities that help to narrow the gap between the rich and the poor, between those who possess skills, knowledge, and technology and those who do not. It is a moral challenge, an invitation to rediscover the truth of the Christian teaching (which is a part of the heritage of the West as well as of the East) that the ultimate test of universal brotherhood lies in the service that is given by man to man because they are brothers.

Relevant to the relations between Europe and Africa, and in fact, to all international relations, is the simple but lofty teaching:

> For I was hungry, and you fed me,
> I was thirsty, and you gave me drink
> I was a stranger, and you entertained me,
> I was unclothed, and you clothed me,
> I was ill, and you looked after me,
> I was in prison, and you visited me.

There are thousands in Africa today who are hungry, for they lack the skills and the technology to deal with the poor soil, the scorching sun that parches the land, the torrential rain that washes it away. There are many who are thirsty, whose women walk miles in the blazing sun to collect, sometimes from muddy and disease-infected ponds, what little water they can carry away; they wait for the skill and the means to bring clean water to their farms and their homes. The African is a stranger, knocking loudly to be admitted as a brother and an equal to the fellowship of man; and in many areas and situations, he is, at best, admitted only through the kitchen door. There are many Africans who are unclothed. And there are many who are ill, fighting incessantly against disease, yet having a life expectancy of no more than thirty years in a land where, for lack of medical aid, men and women die in what should be their prime. And Africans are in prison, in the prison of ignorance and superstition and fear, waiting for the light and freedom that knowledge brings.

It is by loving service and sharing on the basis of common humanity and brotherhood that racial tensions can be resolved. That Christian prescription is unassailable. Every man's soul endorses it, for goodness has its own power to command assent.

The East and the West, instead of carrying the Cold War into Africa, could perhaps find a new basis for mutual trust by working together, pooling their resources and their technology to help Africa. That, too, is a moral question— one on which the peace of the world may well depend. Even though there are African governments ready to pay for what they receive, the challenge to respond is a moral one.

It is quite obvious that there is not enough mutual trust and respect between Africans and Europeans. But there is not enough mutual trust and respect among the nations either, and international diplomacy seems to be conducted on the basis of mutual distrust.

In August, 1960, a conference of career diplomats was held in Switzerland. The participants came from the United States, France, Britain, the Netherlands, Switzerland, the Scandinavian countries, from Russia, Poland, Rumania, Yugoslavia, Czechoslovakia, and from Asia, Africa, and the Middle East. It was truly international and global.

One of the questions discussed was that of disarmament. Representatives from the Soviet Union and those from the Western countries put many searching questions to one another, and some participants who possessed the knowledge went into technical details about nuclear tests, the problems of inspection, and so on; but neither side could fully convince the other as to the appropriate methods of control to be adopted. At the end of several days of exhaustive and frank discussion, one diplomat said, shrugging his shoulders resignedly, "It is very difficult to create confidence."

At one of the closing plenary sessions of the conference, a senior representative of the Soviet Union, a member of the Soviet Academy of Sciences, presented the Soviet view on the Geneva Conference on Disarmament and explained point by point (to those who could follow all the technicalities) what the problems of disarmament were as seen from the Soviet angle. At the end of his erudite address, many questions were put to him; sensing disagreement at one point, he said, in pained and passionate exasperation, "No one will believe us when we say the Soviet Union does not want war and will never start one." The words were spoken with obvious emotion; no amount of scientific detail or diplomatic ingenuity could bypass the moral problems they posed. But high diplomacy seems to overlook the basic things on which normal human relations depend. The degree of distrust and suspicion that underlies attitudes and positions in international affairs was clearly shown in those discussions.

A year later (in August, 1961), Mr. Khrushchev gave a speech in which he himself assured the world that Russia did not want war and would not start one, though he also brandished Russia's undoubted powers of destruction should it have to unleash them. The next day, a London newspaper commented: "The world does not trust Mr. Khrushchev's assurances. This is the crisis of confidence between East and West." An American Congressman was reported to have said, apropos of the same speech: "If you can depend on words, Mr. Khrushchev has spoken more positively than ever before."

The "crisis of confidence between East and West" is fundamentally a moral problem. Because of the lack of mutual trust, there is a tense coexistence, which always threatens to culminate in war. The hope for mankind's survival, unless something better is found, seems to rest on the fact that the East is convinced that the capitalism of the West will collapse, and the West seems to be equally convinced that the Communism of the East is doomed to collapse from within.

If the world cannot find a moral basis for its existence, power and force and conflict must be regarded as the only realistic foundation for national policies and international relations. This is where the new nations of Africa may come in to remind the powerful nations that the true path to harmonious relations and world peace lies in focusing attention on human beings and in going out in a spirit of brotherhood to meet human needs. If East and West joined together to meet the moral challenge to serve the needs of Africa, the most needy continent, they might, through their cooperation to serve a needy brother, rediscover their own brotherhood, and so save humanity.

IV

*THE CHALLENGE
OF RESPONSIBLE EMANCIPATION*

9. *Whither Development?*

THERE are millions of men, women, and children in Africa who need and desire the means to conquer starvation, disease, and ignorance. Their lives portray Africa's lack of skills and equipment, and its poverty. Although many African countries have initiated industries, subsistence agriculture is still the chief occupation and the chief source of income for the majority of the inhabitants of the continent. Africa is mainly a producer and exporter of primary products, agricultural as well as mineral. All the independent states recognize the necessity for rapid economic development.

This is the sphere in which Africa must look to the industrialized countries for help in personnel, finance, technology, and knowledge. This is a sphere in which Africa's own past offers little help.

East and West are now vying with each other to help Africa. An attempt is made here to state what one African, who has had the opportunity to meet intellectuals from both East and West, to speak with them, and to read many of their writings, understands the East and the West to be saying to Africa on the subject of development and the challenges that Africa must face in achieving it.

The Soviet Union and the countries associated with it offer Africa, along with their suggestions as to how the states of Africa should tackle the problem of poverty, their own diagnosis of Africa's situation. Poverty has set the problem of transforming Africa's mainly subsistence economies into modern economies. Soviet writers exhibit a remarkable unanimity on the subject of Africa. All of them make the same diagnosis, and prescribe the same cure. For all take the line that the Marxist-Leninist theory of scientific socialism provides the answer, not only to the problem of poverty, but to all the problems of Africa.

(The case they present is a straightforward one. The backwardness of Africa, in their view, has been created by colonialism. The colonizing powers imposed their capitalist system on Africa. Foreign monopolies exploited Africa, and took away its wealth. Hence the prevailing poverty in Africa.)

The Soviet Union understands the problems of Africa, and because of its own experience, it can help Africa. Russia faced and successfully solved the problem of rapid economic development. Moreover, in the Soviet Union, there are countries, such as Kazakh and the Moslem republics of Soviet Central Asia, that had conditions similar to those in Africa —poverty, ignorance, illiteracy. Guided by Marxist-Leninist theory, these countries have pulled themselves out of their poverty and up to prosperity. They provide examples of the successful application of Marxist-Leninist theory to the problem of development. The Soviet Union has the instruments and experience for the rapid modernization of an underdeveloped country.

Marxist-Leninist theory is as applicable to Africa as to any other country. History shows an unmistakable transition from capitalism to socialism, as Marx foretold. The theory provides a scientific interpretation of social development. It shows that social development is founded on the mode of production. The entire social system and its political, juridical, philosophical, religious, literary, and aesthetic institutions are, in the final analysis, determined by the mode of production.

A country is underdeveloped when, like Africa, its industry is poorly developed. Economic progress can be founded only on industry. All other problems can be solved when that has been done. But without industrial development, it is impossible to have economic progress.

Marxist-Leninist theory makes it quite clear that if countries in Africa want to achieve economic progress, they must concentrate on improving production. This means they must industrialize; and real economic independence requires that such industrialization should include the manufacturing of the means of production, the development of heavy industry. To overcome its poverty, this is what Africa must do, and it must be done as rapidly as possible.

It is allowed that not every country in Africa has the resources for setting up heavy industry. But all can and must have light industry to supply consumer goods.

The key words for progress are industrialization, nationalization, and cooperation. Africa is still largely an agricultural country. Agricultural productivity must be increased. This cannot be done without more efficient tools; plows and tractors are needed; agriculture must be mechanized. Such mechanization is beyond the means of the individual farmer; cooperatives must be formed. The tradition of joint ownership of land and cooperative work on it is, of course, a very old one in many African communities. This tradition helps producer cooperatives, but the new form of cooperation has to be guided by government.

In fact, the whole exercise implies a transition to a socialist society. For this, it is essential to have a proletariat, and a lively class-consciousness. There are some who may think that the Marxist-Leninist prescription does not apply to Africa because Africa has no class structure. But recent Soviet authors have been at pains to show that African society is not without its class structure. In traditional African structures, they have found a mixture of tribal, feudal, and capitalist elements; in the modern sections of Africa, they have noted the emergence of a a proletariat, a national bourgeoisie, and a rising intelligentsia—classes corresponding to those in capitalist societies. It would, therefore, be a mistake for anyone to suppose that Marxist-Leninist theory does not apply to Africa.

The development of a proletariat and the development of class consciousness are evidently of vital importance for scientific socialism; for, according to Soviet authorities, a socialist state is one in which state authority is in the hands of the proletariat, the means of production are publicly owned, and there is no exploitation of one class by another, or of one man by another. Further, in a socialist state, economic development is planned, controlled, and directed by the state. If a country wants rapid economic development, it must follow the road of nationalization and central planning.

It is clear that development in accordance with Marxist-Leninist theory means development within the framework of a socialist state, and any African state that chooses that way has the model of the Soviet Union to follow. It must, like the Soviet Union, have a government that has the necessary instruments of coercion and control, not only to ensure its own rule, but also to impose the discipline that will be required in a single-minded and resolute drive for industrialization, the essential foundation for all progress, material and spiritual. This is the case that Soviet writers put to Africa with much force and conviction.

Not guided by a common doctrine, such as Soviet writers have in Marxist-Leninism, the West speaks to Africa in many voices. Western writers have but little unanimity in their approach to the problems of economic development in Africa. No Western writer claims that either he or some acknowledged genius has discovered the infallible theory that explains history and social development and is applicable to all times and peoples. Everyone is agreed on the need for economic development. What Western writers present is an ongoing search, an interchange of ideas, a veritable clash of minds in the quest for understanding and for solutions.

To begin with, there is a search for understanding of the meaning and implications of the very concept of underdevelopment which is now in general use. It is applied to countries in Africa, Asia, Latin America, and even to certain regions of highly industrialized countries. In each instance, its application indicates the presence of one or more of the following characteristics: the productivity of human labor is low, as is the national or per capita income; the instruments of production consist of tools rather than machines; the majority of the people are engaged in agriculture rather than industry; the greater proportion of them are rural and live in villages and small towns rather than cities; there is generally a high rate of illiteracy; both birth and death rates are comparatively high; social structures tend to be stable and rigid, and there is little social mobility. But so widely do the different countries classified as "underdeveloped" vary in fulfilling, and not fulfilling, these criteria that some writers question whether any precise definition can be given to the concept.

There is, however, general agreement on the narrower concept of economic development, which is conceded always to imply the establishment of an economy in which productivity is high and the national or per capita income is also high. But is this to be the sole aim of development?

The programs different underdeveloped countries have designed for economic growth have often been accompanied by programs of social welfare—programs for achieving "a richer life" or for "improving the lot of the people." These development plans take account of aspects of social life other than the economic and aim at more than just increasing productivity. They raise questions of planning as well as of methods. Can there be a general line of development for all countries? Should development plans stress heavy industry in order to achieve a rapid expansion of productive capacity? Or should more emphasis be placed on consumer industries? Which is the quicker way to absorb idle hands? To raise living standards? How should economic growth be most effectively stimulated? Through government planning? Through the free operation of market forces? Or through some judicious mixture of both? These and a host of similar questions have been asked. Attempts at answers show a great deal of disagreement, indicative of the search and of free inquiry. The proposals as to methods, for example, range from suggestions for completely planned economies, with governments making all the major decisions, as does the Soviet Government, to suggestions that governments provide only the funds for basic social improvements, leaving the rest to private capital and enterprise.

There are, among Western writers, democratic socialists who hold, like the Soviet writers, that capitalism is inefficient and does not yield the rapid increases in production that should be possible with the methods and the machinery contemporary technology provides. These writers also maintain that capitalism is unjust because it leads to an uneven—and unfair—distribution of wealth and income. But, unlike the Soviet writers, they contend that socialism can and should be achieved, not through coercion or revolution, but through a series of gradual reforms realized by means of parliamentary democracy.

What, then, is the model recommended for Africa to follow? The West offers no dogmatic or unanimous answer.

Empirically, it searches for different answers, applicable in different situations.

Some authorities have held that underdeveloped countries in Africa must adopt not only the economic and technological methods of the industrialized West but also its social structures and even its political systems. They contend that economic development is possible for underdeveloped countries only if their social relations are modeled on those of Western capitalist nations. There is no need, they argue, to worry about the traditional cultures and values of Africa —the scientific, technological revolution will sweep them all away.

Others hold an opposite view. They admit that, with industrialization and the adoption of modern techniques and skills and machinery, there will be profound changes in the social structures of African societies. But, they maintain, this should not, and need not, destroy Africa's cultures. Whether or not it does depends on the choices Africans make and the leadership African countries are given. If the process of development is to be properly guided, it is necessary to have adequate knowledge not only of technological factors and processes but also of social factors and processes and of the goals or ends toward which development is to be directed.

Despite their diversity of views, Western writers are consistently in agreement on one point—that economic growth should not override but should be reconciled with human dignity and freedom. The way to be sought is one that secures freedom as well as adequate economic growth.

Both Soviet and Western writers seem to agree that neither production nor consumption is an end in itself, that development is primarily concerned with human beings, with their well-being, their place in society, and their relations with their fellow men. For this reason, increased productivity cannot be the sole consideration in the process of development. The focus on human beings must have a bearing on what is produced, on how it is produced, and also on how it is distributed.

It is important to consider whether what is produced at a particular time is the best product or combination of products for human well-being, or whether increased production is being achieved at the cost of living standards; whether production is being carried on by methods and through social organizations that enhance human dignity and freedom, or whether by methods and through organizations that sacrifice them for increased productivity; whether what is produced is justly shared, or whether it enriches a few at the expense of the many. It is possible to have economic growth in the sense of increased production without the majority of the people being better off. The increase may benefit a powerful few—and cost the majority their freedom.

Though there is discernible agreement between East and West (as judged from authors on either side) that the well-being and social relations of human beings should be the primary consideration, and that it is therefore important and relevant to consider what is produced, how it is produced, and how it is distributed on that basis, there is disagreement as to the application and interpretation of these principles. For questions of what should be produced, and how it should be produced, and how it should be shared go beyond material welfare into the values and goals of society.

Social development must be related to the goals of society —to what the individuals in the society deem to be desirable for themselves and for the community in which they live. This again reaches into the sphere of morals. It is related to what the society and its members think to be the good life.

This brief survey summarizes the principal ideas and

goals that the industrial countries of Europe and the United States, of the Western and of the Eastern bloc, present to the states of Africa eager to develop their resources as quickly as possible.

The African countries are making their choices; they are in the process of establishing new systems. In the particular circumstances of Africa, governments are already playing leading roles in industrial development. Systems of communications are governmentally owned; large enterprises are being established with state funds, or jointly with state and private capital; and development is directed by government plans. But many African governments have expressed the need for outside investment, and the readiness to welcome it on favorable terms.

As has been noted, the tradition of joint ownership of land and cooperative work on that land exists in many African communities. This traditionally corporate life has emphasized group solidarity rather than individualism. Individualism is a new phenomenon, one of the indices of the social changes resulting from the impact of technology, commerce, industry, and new ideas. In view of this tradition, and of the role of governments, some of the leaders of African states have pointed out that their respective countries are traditionally socialist rather than capitalist.

Liberia is not one of the states that claim to be following a socialist policy; and therefore, special attention must be given to the official statement made by Liberia's Secretary of the Treasury at a Conference in Nigeria in 1960 that "in view of the long tradition of communalism in Africa, strong adulterations must be made to any individualistic and impersonal system that is prescribed for Africa." Liberia's proclaimed policy is one of economic cooperation between private capital and government working together to an economic system that will hasten development but that will not, in the process, destroy the liberties of the people.

There have, in Africa, been avowals of socialism with varying connotations. President Senghor of Senegal has expressed the view that African communities were socialist before they were colonized by European powers, and that what is called for is the re-establishment of African socialist states on new bases. President Nasser of Egypt has declared a policy of building a cooperative socialist society that will also be democratic. The official policies of Ghana, Guinea, and Mali call for the creation of socialist states. Nyerere, former Prime Minister of Tanganyika, seeks a social system that will express the concern of the government for the welfare of the masses. But "African socialism," "cooperative socialism," and "scientific socialism" do not mean the same thing, and there are wide and fundamental differences in the organizational structures, the methods, and the goals of the different countries that have declared their policies to be socialist. They are not all following the Soviet model; while some are obviously pulled in the Soviet direction, or pledge their allegiance to Marxism, others are plowing their own way in search of a balance between economic development and freedom. Communism and democracy are both magnets, each exercising its attraction.

But the challenge must be faced. It is in relation to the answer to the question "Whither development?" that choices should be made. The chosen goal should be clear. The ultimate test should be the quality of life and the sort of society that the development plans are intended to achieve.

The crucial problem is the quality of the individual member of society. How it is answered will depend on the opportunities he has to develop himself, and on the sort of society in which he lives. More food, housing, clothing, more and better services, more education, and so on—all of these and all of the amenities that contemporary civilization places within reach are sought in order that the quality of individual and social life may be better. Good social conditions give men and women a better chance to improve the quality of their lives—to live the good life as they understand it. There may be different conceptions of the good life, but all men desire freedom. All over Africa, in all of its villages and in all of its towns, men, women, and children crave freedom.

Development plans should be inspired and conditioned by the desire to give every citizen, every man, woman and child, the best chance a country can give for a full, happy, and useful life. This can only be attained in freedom. It is possible to achieve high productivity and high national or per capita income by methods that destroy human dignity and freedom—by methods of subjection. People can be forced to work and to forgo their basic needs, forced to save, and forced to yield to crippling measures of governmental control in order to increase productivity.

But the goal of economic, and social, development is the freedom and uplift of the individual and the improvement of human relations and the quality of social life. This is the challenge that African nations must face in their choice of methods to tackle the problem of development. Neither productivity nor consumption is an end in itself.

10. African Cultures and the Challenge of Industrialization

THE discussion in the previous chapter shows that, for Africa, the problem of development is closely connected with the problem of industrialization. The rich countries are industrialized; to become rich, African countries must also become industrialized. There are indeed some rich countries, like Denmark, New Zealand and Canada, that are regarded as agricultural countries; but the fact is that they all derive more income from the things they manufacture than from primary products. Most African countries, on the other hand, are dependent on primary products for the greater part of their national incomes.

As a country becomes industrialized, more and more of its working population is diverted from agriculture to manufacture—from the farm to shops and factories. In all industrialized countries, industrialization has resulted in more of the national product originating in factories than on farms. With this change, there has been a corresponding fall in the number of people who are engaged in agriculture. For example, in 1850, 70 per cent of the working population of the United States was engaged in agriculture; 100 years later, only 15 per cent of the working population was engaged in agriculture, but technological advances had made it possible for this much smaller share of the population to increase agricultural production by more than 250 per cent as compared with 1850; and so, though the proportion of the working population employed in agriculture was much reduced, it could provide for a much larger population.

When an agricultural country sets out to industrialize, it starts on a path that means immediate changes in occupations for many of its citizens. This, in turn, affects many aspects of social life, for changes in occupations lead to changes in personalities and in human relations, and to new social groupings. Industrialization in Africa, as has been shown in many studies already undertaken, is changing the kinship structures of traditional societies.

Industrialization is not only a factor in cultural change; it is also an outcome of the process of culture change. There is a constantly operating relationship between human interaction and the occupational patterns and technology of a society; they are interdependent, and social organizations change as a consequence of changes in occupations and technology. Thus, behind the desire for industrialization, looms the question of what will happen to African cultures as the countries of Africa become industrialized in order to raise national incomes and standards of living.

Some of the cherished values of these cultures must change if a social framework favorable for industrialization is to be created. In the agricultural subsistence economies of Africa many are self-employed. Though productivity is low, the men have much freedom in the use of their time. They make their own decisions about when to start work, when to stop, when to take time off; they work when and as they please. The use of time is governed by a scale of values in which income and productivity do not rank as high as they do in an industrial society. Visiting relations, attending funerals, and participating in community festivals often rank much higher than increasing production or accumulating wealth. Industrialization calls for a revaluation and a new hierarchical arrangement of social values. In particular, the desire for wealth and the will to economize must rank high. Such changes are already taking place in Africa. A greater incentive to work and effort now springs from the desire to acquire material wealth, for material wealth has become an avenue to social prestige and power. This is one of the indices of change in traditional evaluations and cultures.

Traditional positions of power and prestige are rivaled by new roles (with higher status) that can now be achieved through success in economic activities. Consequently, the transition toward an industrial society is marked by a change in which there is a closer correlation between income or wealth and social status.

This and other changes have to take place if industrialization is to be successful. The people must learn new ways and accept new values. A counterpart of this change is what some economists refer to as the need for "commitment." They point out that if industrialization is to proceed successfully, there must be a labor force fully "committed" to industrial work. This really means that workers must learn not only new skills but also new ways. They must accept the cultural values of an industrial system, the discipline that industrial work imposes, and the rewards it offers as an incentive to work. This implies changes in the cultural values of a traditional African society, where prestige attaches to spending, where the obligations to generosity and hospitality, especially to one's kinsfolk, encourage spending rather than saving, where conspicuous consumption rather than productive investment is the avenue to social esteem and prestige.

Not only the learning of new skills but the acceptance of new values is necessary for increased production. But the old pattern of social relations, including family and kinship obligations, cannot be fulfilled when the new values are accepted. The values of a "committed" labor force in an industrial system are incompatible with some of the values of a culture unit in a subsistence economy.

The new skills that have to be learned afford opportunities for different modes of earning a living, for variety, and for specialization. The inequality in earnings that results fosters the development of a new social stratification. Industrialization and economic growth have been marked by the emergence and growing importance of a middle class. Social stratification in industrialized countries, such as Britain, the United States, the Netherlands, France, West Germany, Switzerland, and the Scandinavian lands, attests to the importance of the middle class, which grows to provide the essential services of an industrial civilization. In the developing countries of Africa the same process is discernible. There is an emergence of the skilled executive and administrative personnel that industrialization demands. This, in turn, reflects new social relations and, consequently, cultural change.

Units organized for production in factory, mine, or shop, or to operate the bureaucratic machinery for a town or heterogeneous group, are different in size, function, and composition from families or tribes. The emergence of new social groups and associations, catering to different interests, attests to a culture different from one in which the all-embracing net of kinship relations met every need of social life.

Industrialization is associated with the growth of towns. Though most of Africa's population is still rural, the evidence is that new towns are springing up and old ones are growing. The town population is increasing. The growing towns of Africa mirror its changing cultures. A town is inhabited by people from many different communities, often even from many different countries. In the town, the growth of many different functional associations, serving many different interests, attests to the decreasing influence of kinship groups—or their inability to cope with the new conditions of town life. The town's police and its law courts, for example, illustrate the new social sanctions that are necessary to bring order to a heterogeneous community. Loyalty to family traditions no longer suffices to ensure good social behavior; in fact, there is, in many towns, a manifest absence of continuity about what constitutes good social behavior. More and more laws are required to regulate social behavior—these laws are another index of culture change.

The housing, occupations, the different modes of living that a town exhibits, in their multiplicity and variety, give evidence of continuous cultural change. There are more alternative patterns and choices of associations, institutions, and occupations.

One of the most striking differences between tribal African communities and industrial societies lies in their respective communication systems. A tribal community lives in comparative isolation. Its means of communication are laborious and slow, and can reach only a few people at a time. Social communication is primarily through the spoken word, and the normal way of transmitting information over a distance is to send a messenger, on foot or horseback, but more often on foot. There is also an extensive use of nonverbal symbols of communication, such as gestures or, in the dance, bodily motions that have specific meanings intelligible to those who are familiar with the particular culture. These are prized aspects of African cultures. Messages may also be conveyed by smoke or fire signals, or by drums; but if a distance of about fifteen miles is reached by these means, it is considered a great achievement.

Only comparatively small audiences can be reached, and a very limited amount of information can be conveyed through these media. The people in a tribal village or town can be assembled only through messengers, or a town crier using the human voice, a horn, a drum, or a gong; no audience can consist of more people than these instruments can reach.

Where the means of communications are poor, the pace of culture change tends to be very slow. The people develop an intense loyalty to local traditions, for new ideas, from outside, are few and far between. The degree of conformity is high, and social contacts are predominantly primary, or face to face.

One of the necessary requirements of successful industrialization is improvement in communications. The introduction of new systems of communication into African communities has helped to quicken the pace of social change. Better communications in the form of roads or railways make for greater physical contacts between people; the telephone and the telegraph make it possible to transmit messages much more quickly; the cinema, the loud speaker, the radio convey ideas and information to many more people. Tribal isolation is broken; larger and more heterogeneous communities emerge, and wider opportunities and choices become available.

Of the changes that took place in communication media in the United States during the nineteenth century, Charles Cooley, an American sociologist, observed that "the change to the present regime of railroads, telegraphs, daily papers, telephones, and the rest has involved a revolution in every phase of life; in commerce, in politics, in education, even in sociability and gossip—this revolution always consisting in an enlargement and quickening of the kind of life in question."* Similar enlargement and animation can be documented from the development of communications in Africa.

There is a general recognition that the mass media of contemporay civilization are powerful tools for the trans-

* *Social Organization* (Glencoe, Ill.: The Free Press, 1955), p. 83.

formation of whole societies. The essential feature of communications, however, is that one person, by speech, gesture, or other symbols, tries to convey an idea or feeling to another. For social contact, the idea or feeling has to be understood, and acknowledged by an appropriate reaction or response. This requires the use of a language that is understood by those with whom one wishes to communicate. For communicating with African communities, this means the use of their own vernacular languages. But the use of vernacular languages poses challenges and problems. Within the boundaries of a small state, dozens of languages may be spoken by the various tribes that compose the new nation.

Linguists tell us that there are more than 800 different languages spoken in tropical Africa. Many of them have no written forms as yet. Both for reasons of economy and in order to reach wider audiences, it is necessary to use fewer languages. Radio, press, and literary campaigns offer opportunities to spread the understanding and use of a selected number of vernacular languages. This is one aspect of the problem of nation building in some of the new states of Africa. It is also a problem of industrialization.

Heterogeneity and urbanization accompany industrialization. People from different tribes come to live together in mining centers and factory towns, and vernacular languages must meet the new situation. The challenge is being met, in that certain vernacular languages are extending beyond their original tribal boundaries and are being learned and used by other tribes; but this is a development that calls for conscious choices, conscious decisions.

Industrialization, by increasing heterogeneity and quickening culture changes, offers a richer life and a wider range of choices. The benefits of industrialization are accompanied by profound changes in traditional ways of life.

In a paper on "The Achievement Motive in Economic

Growth," presented at the North American Conference on the Social Consequences of Industrialization (held in Chicago in 1960), Professor David McClelland wrote:

> Western and Eastern intellectuals both frequently observe that they sincerely hope the East can develop economically without losing the many valuable features of its existing way of life and institutions; without becoming "materialistic" like the West. To a certain extent such statements, while admirable in many ways, are simply incompatible with the psychological requirements for a modern society. For instance, peacefulness and calm acceptance of life as it occurs are virtues the East might well wish to maintain, and the West to acquire, but it is surely nonsense to think one can maintain those values and at the same time develop a nation of bustling entre- preneurs whose vigorous efforts are absolutely essential to economic advance.

For Africa, just as for the East, industrialization is ac- companied by changes in some institutions, some beliefs, habits, and values. Because such profound changes take place, the question is raised, To what extent can one speak of African cultures in the context of industrialization and rapid social change? For, in that context, the old bonds of family and tribe are weakened or have to be expressed in new forms; new political institutions and social structures emerge; old customs are replaced by new norms. Is it pos- sible, in the face of all this, to contend that African cultures continue to have valid identities of their own?

New ways must always be seen in the context of the old. The changes a society accepts at any given time are small relative to its total culture. There is always opportunity for a new cultural pattern borrowed from outside to be molded by the borrowers to make it fit into their own cultural milieu; in that sense, the borrowed cultural pattern becomes their own. So we may study Christianity or Islam or ballroom dancing or human relations in an industrial plant in Africa, and discover that they have been endowed with new patterns, deriving from the cultures into which they have been incorporated. A new musical instrument may be accepted, but it will probably be used to play tunes that fit into the rhythmic and all the other musical traditions of those who have borrowed it; ballroom dancing may be borrowed, but the quick multiple rhythms of "high life" may replace the gainly waltz; Christianity or Islam may gain loyal converts, but they will gather accretions stemming from the borrowers' own traditional concepts of the universe; new scientific techniques may be learned, but explanations of certain phenomena and certain experiences will still be sought in magical or spiritual terms—not because, as some aver, Africans have no idea of causality in natural phenomena, but because some questions are posed in the context of a cultural tradition in a form that science cannot answer; science narrows but does not abrogate the sphere of the supernatural. All cultures change; particular customs, institutions, or ideas that are borrowed are molded into the existing culture; there are different possible combinations of cultural complexes, and the choices made reflect a people's own culture. For, in the context of culture, we are not dealing with forces that operate independently of human will. There are indeed limiting conditions imposed by the particular historical and social situation, but there is always room for conscious choices. Culture change is a selective process. Earlier ways can be dropped, or adapted and retained in changed forms; new ways can be accepted and fitted into old ones.

The search by Africans for greater knowledge of their own traditional cultures, their languages, history, customs, arts and crafts, folklore, music, religious systems, beliefs, and values stems from the assumption that such knowledge will help them the better to deal with their own problems of cultural selection and retention, with their own problems of culture change. It arises from the awakened national consciousness that it is through an enlightened devotion to their own ways of life that they will make their own contribution to the emergent world community into which they seek admission and acceptance on terms of equality. As the committee of experts convened by UNESCO put it: "The problem of international understanding is the problem of the relations of cultures. From those relations must emerge a new world community of understanding and mutual respect."*

This is the implicit basis for the new preoccupation of African nationals with their own cultures. In a sense, the distinctive and unique aspects of African cultures give proof of the genius and dignity of the African. The preoccupation is thus a part of the quest for acceptance as equals and for the recognition of the dignity of the African. It is an aspect of nationalism. But the quest both for African cultures and for industrialization demands a greater knowledge of social processes and of the degree to which human choice and control may be exercised on the processes of social change. Planning is based on the assumption that some choice and control is possible, for industrialization as well as for the culture as a whole.

* *Interrelations of Culture* (Paris: UNESCO, 1953).

11. The Challenge of Nationalism

AFRICAN nationalism throws many challenges, some to countries outside Africa, especially the colonial powers, and some to the leaders and peoples of Africa. Some of these challenges have been apparent throughout the problems we have discussed.

The fact that African nationalism is, in the first place, a demand for racial equality is its most conspicuous attribute. Africans demand acceptance as equals in the human family.

This has political dimensions, because colonialism in Africa has been marked by the domination of Africans by Europeans. So the demand for equality finds expression in the demand for the emancipation of all Africa from colonial rule. That is a challenge which African nationalism throws to the European powers that have colonies in Africa.

The demand for emancipation from colonial rule is a demand for national independence; that does not by itself give personal freedom to the individual citizen. The challenge to provide the kind of government that guarantees individual freedom is one thrown to the rulers of the independent states of Africa by their own compatriots. The challenge is also thrown by those outside Africa who, observing the trends in independent African states, contend that democracy is not suited to Africa and that the peoples of Africa themselves prefer authoritarian rule.

That challenge cannot be lightly brushed aside. There are trends that give cause for the contention. One who surveys the independent states of Africa can make an impressive list of these trends: in some states, no opposition parties, or only emasculated ones; a marked growth of monolithic one-party rule; countries in which ruling parties are swallowing up the trade unions, youth organizations, farmers' councils, women's federations, civil servants and other associations—and where one must hold a party card before one can expect to be employed; trends toward one-man rule, and even a personality cult; government or party control of the media of communication, particularly of the press and radio; arbitrary arrests and imprisonment of political opponents without trial; attacks on the independence of the judiciary, or interference with the impartial administration of the law.

There are factors that favor such trends, particularly in newly independent states, just emerged from colonialism. At independence, as already stated, the machinery of government that the new African governments take over is authoritarian; colonial rule engenders subservience to authority, and this can and has been exploited. Often there is no effective public opinion, or no vehicle for its expression; for the institutions—the voluntary societies, trade unions, professional associations, and so on—that, in democratic countries, protect various rights and interests or serve as vehicles for the effective expression of public opinion are either non-existent, or where they exist are government-sponsored or can be quickly brought under control. Where there are elections to the legislature or councils, it is easy to rig them, for the majority of the citizens are illiterate.

In some states, ethnic or regional or local interests rallied people together to demand what they conceived to be their rights or to resist encroachments on such rights. But such resistances can easily be discredited as reactionary tribalism, whose suppression is a creditable act of nation building.

There is the need for rapid economic development. The task set is to raise living standards to the extent resources and available skills make possible. We have, in this connection, discussed the case presented by those who advocate development in accordance with Marxist-Leninist theory. In practice, it teaches, even demands, the establishment of one-party rule, with pressures to bring trade unions and all other organizations into the ruling party as the best way to achieve economic development. Marxist-Leninism directs development through a monolithic party. It has had its appeal and impact on trends in some of the new states in Africa.

Would-be investors from Western democracies, as we have pointed out, demand strong governments, and thus encourage the development of authoritarian rule.

Even in the old democracies of Europe and America, political scientists have observed trends toward one-man rule as a characteristic development of the present century—the emergence of the heroic leader. The fact is that the increasing role of government in economic affairs, or in establishing the welfare state, or in dealing with international crises in a world whose parts have become increasingly interdependent, tends to strengthen the power of government in a way that constitutes a threat to democracy, even where there are established traditions and institutions to restrain authoritarian tendencies.

In Africa, where parliamentary institutions are new, and where there is such a massive preponderance of conditions favoring authoritarian rule, the battle for personal liberty and democracy is a hard one, with the odds heavily against the few who are fighting it. It has better chances of success where the leaders in power set themselves to establish true democracy and to respect civil liberties. It is a severe moral test calling for wisdom and tolerance. It is well-known that people in power tend to be corrupted by it; at least they do everything they can to remain in power. So it should be recognized that the circumstances under which the battle for personal freedom and democracy has to be fought in Africa are difficult; nevertheless, they do not offer any evidence for the conclusion that democracy is unworkable in Africa, or that the civil liberties stressed as essential in democratic countries are not applicable to Africans.

Independence is coming to Africa at a time and under circumstances that make it easy for governments to be authoritarian and even totalitarian, if they choose to go that way. But none of the prevailing circumstances that are favorable to the establishment of authoritarian rule are unalterable. Personal freedom constitutes a challenge to African nationalism.

The principles of democracy—freedom of speech, including the right to criticize and to propagandize against the government; freedom of assembly and association, including the freedom to organize opposition parties and to propose alternative governments; freedom of the people to choose their government at general elections, and to change them peacefully; freedom of religion; freedom from arbitrary arrest and imprisonment without trial; the rule of law; guarantees for human rights and civil liberties—all these principles of parliamentary government are universal. They can be adopted and applied by any nation that chooses to do so. They can be institutionalized in any culture.

The choice has to be made by the African states. There are leaders of African states who have accepted these principles and are determined to adhere to them. It is a challenge to African leaders to justify their claim for freedom and to give evidence of their maturity by making their states citadels of freedom, national and individual. African nationalism demands of others, in the challenge it throws for emancipation of Africa from colonial rule, justice, respect for human rights and human dignity, wisdom, tact, patience, and integrity. The establishment of democracy in Africa, the guarantee and extension of human rights and personal freedom to the citizens of Africa, justifiably call for the display of the same standards of conduct from Africans. It is a challenge that cannot be evaded; but it must be admitted that those who are trying to meet it are in the minority.

African nationalism is also a demand for cultural freedom. In this context, we have discussed the concepts of African personality and Negritude in their various aspects—as a revolt against colonialism, as a demand for respect and recognition of equality, and as attempts to find an emotional and cultural base for African unity, already given political expression in Pan-Africanism.

The contemporary technology, the international, interdependent economic life, and the threat of annihilation that hangs over the human species—all compel nations to find ways of coming closer together. There is a search going on to find a common moral language to bind them into a world community. Part of the search finds expression in the larger and larger unions of nations that are being formed all over the world.

The vision of a united African nation can be traced back to the yearnings and dreams of Africans who were exported as slaves to work in plantations in the United States and the West Indies. They dreamed of repatriation to the homeland, which in their dreams was just Mother Africa, one homeland, not many nations. With the abolition of the slave trade, and the manumission of slaves in America and the West Indies, the return to the nation of Africa became more than a dream. It became a quest for something realizable. Over the years, the quest has gathered momentum, and with the emergence of many more independent states in Africa, and the compulsions to larger unions, it has now come to constitute a challenge to African nationalism.

The future of Africa, and Africa's role in the future of the world, depend upon the divisions or groupings that take place on the continent, upon its Balkanization, or integration. But there are formidable problems to be faced in the quest for the Union of Africa, and there are different views on the approaches and steps to it. First, a look at some of the problems.

There are independent states in which the component groups have still to be mobilized into a nation; colonial administration has given an administrative framework but not the inner unity of nationhood. This task has first to be completed.

African states have been formed within the geographical boundaries arbitrarily drawn by colonial powers. These boundaries create illogical frontiers, separating ethnic and linguistic groups, and even families. There are states in Central, East, and West Africa between which the seeds of Irredentism have been sown by the Conference of Berlin of 1885, and subsequent delimitations of possessions and trust territories among European powers after World War I. This is another task calling for attention and statesmanship.

There are racial, linguistic, and cultural differences, complicated by the divergent influences of colonial powers. Some African states have closer links with France or Britain, to whom they owe their introduction to European technology, to new ideas and political systems and culture, than they have with neighboring territories in Africa. These links are strengthened by economic and financial ties, as well as by communications and military alliances. Ghana, Nigeria, Sierra Leone, and Tanganyika belong to the Commonwealth, as do the British colonies that are not yet self-governing: Gambia, Kenya, Nyasaland, and the Rhodesias. All of these, and also Libya and South Africa, belong to the sterling area. The Central African Republic and the republics of Chad, the Congo (Brazzaville), Gabon, Malagasy, and Senegal are members of the French Community, with which Cameroun, Dahomey, Ivory Coast, Niger, Togo, and Upper Volta are associated through agreements. All these states are also members of the franc zone, to which Morocco and Mali belong on terms that permit them to exercise control over financial transfers.

There are problems of military alliances, defense, and military bases about which different states have separate and different agreements or understandings with Britain or France, and which some of them consider it would be unsafe to give up.

These are some of the hurdles on the way to African unity. Given time and good will, they are not unsurmountable. With regard to the linguistic and cultural differences, for example, contemporary media of communication offer opportunities for achieving cultural homogeneity; for cultures can be learned. Economic considerations aid the creation of a large union with a diversity of agricultural and mineral resources. At present, however, the absence or paucity of communications and economic links between African states must be counted among the handicaps.

Approaches to unity can be along the line of cooperation in realizing shared interests and limited goals, or by voluntary associations pragmatic in character, or by political unions, voluntary or imposed. Differences in approach have led to the existence of two separate groupings. At the beginning of 1962, these were: the Casablanca Powers, consisting of the Algerian Provisional Government, Ghana, Guinea, Mali, Morocco, and the United Arab Republic; and the larger group, the Monrovia Powers, consisting of Cameroun, the Central African Republic, Chad, Congo (Brazzaville), Congo (Léopoldville), Dahomey, Ethiopia, Gabon, Ivory

Coast, Liberia, Malagasy, Mauritania, Niger, Senegal, Sierra Leone, Somalia, Togo, Tunisia, and Upper Volta. Besides their ideological differences, discernible if not explicit, the Casablanca group appears to place more emphasis on political union as a vehicle to unity, while the Monrovia group has an empirical approach to political unity to be gained through the cooperation of sovereign states for realizing common interests and objectives. An examination of the recommendations of committees set up by the respective groups to consider the implementation of their objectives show them to be nearer in their objectives than press vitriolics from one side against the other would indicate. The recommendations of experts of the Casablanca group meeting in Conakry (Guinea) in 1961 included the establishment of a common market, ending of quota systems between the states, the establishment of a council of African economic unity and an African economic development bank. The committee of the Monrovia Powers which met in Dakar (Senegal), also in 1961, recommended, among other things, setting up a regional customs union, establishing a common external tariff, building a network of communications to connect the states and foster the exchange of information, and founding an African development bank and an investment fund. At the Lagos Conference of January, 1962, these countries advanced their proposals for cooperation in economic and cultural fields.

Ideological differences are implicit in the stipulations of the Monrovia Powers that the sovereignty of each state should be respected, whether it is a large state or a small one; that the principle of noninterference in the internal affairs of each state should be observed; that each state should have the right to federate with any other African state.

In addition to the two groups, regional unions and associations are being formed on the basis of geographical, cultural, political, and economic interests. At the beginning of 1962, there were the Ghana-Guinea-Mali Union; the Conseil de l'Entente, consisting of the republics of Dahomey, Ivory Coast, and Upper Volta; and the Union des Républiques d'Afrique Centrale, which comprised the Central African Republic and the republics of Chad and the Congo (Brazzaville). Their character and forms of relationship varied a good deal. Other unions or associations are being discussed in West as well as East Africa. The formation of regional unions and associations of contiguous states turns out to be more practicable and realistic at the present stage, since it appears to be the more realizable preliminary step toward a union of African states.

A discussion of the problems of African union cannot be confined to the Negroid race, nor can the continent be isolated from the rest of the world. The extent to which states in Africa should continue political, economic, or cultural associations with former colonial powers is one of the questions on which there are differences between the various African states. Some consider that any form of association between an independent African state and the former colonial power is a retention of the vestiges of colonialism; others do not think so. Links with Europe have therefore become controversial; yet Africa cannot ignore its ties with Europe. There are the contributions Europe has made to Africa's culture, to its technology, and to its political and economic life. There are independent states in Africa where English or French is the medium of communication between the different tribes that make up the state. French and English are also the means of communication between different African states, and with peoples outside Africa. In these fields, Europe has made enduring contributions to Africa, as Africa has made to Europe in other fields.

There are links with other countries outside Africa besides the colonial powers which affect African unity. The

Pan-Arab League and the Islamic religion draw some of the peoples of Africa into close associations with others outside the continent.

Moreover, Africa is now an active member of the international society of nations. African nationalism does not only represent moral indignation against injustice and wrong, against the degradation of slavery, colonial subjection, discrimination, and apartheid; it is also a claim for equality. The latter must carry with it the obligation to share the common responsibility for the common good of the human family. African nationalism challenges the peoples of Africa to seek opportunities to demonstrate their maturity and equality, and to win respect through cooperation, and through their own distinctive contributions to the welfare of mankind and to world peace. This is why organizations like the United Nations receive their support. The fulfillment of their new obligations require the forging or maintenance of mutually beneficial and friendly links with other peoples, the former colonial powers included; for all nations have to share in the building of a world community that ensures world peace; and that calls for the cooperation of all races.

Thus, the quest for a Union of African States faces many problems—technical, political, and cultural. There are problems of defense and military alliances; of securing human rights and freedom for all; of forging links with other cultures and peoples. But the crucial problem is man himself. In Africa, as in Europe, unity and concord are hindered, above everything else, by suspicion and distrust. Between the different states of Africa there are some wide gulfs of mistrust, dug by the activities of some ambitious leaders. There is also stockpiling of arms in Africa; guns and ammunition pass secretly across frontiers; saboteurs trained in one state have been sent into another to distribute money and arms to topple the governments of other states. Plots have been discovered, and there is constant suspicion of new plots. These are greater dangers to peace and unity than the open problems to which men of good will can in time find solutions and accommodating compromises.

The problems of a nation, even a small one, cannot all be solved in the life span of any one man, or even in any one generation. The problems of Africa belong to many generations of men. The mountains that loom so formidably today will be distant hillocks behind the generations of tomorrow. But overweening ambition to erect what they think will be their own immortal monuments drives some men in tempestuous haste to telescope all history into one lifetime, and they seek to destroy in the process all who will not submit to their imperious will. So they sow the seeds of discord, suspicion, and fear. In human history the seeds of discord bear fruit in conflagrations in which not only overweening ambition but also precious lives are scorched or burned out. It is not given to man to make himself immortal. It will take more than a lifetime to build a united nation out of the states of Africa. The vision was seen 300 years ago, in the darkest days of slavery. It has come nearer to reality since then; but it is not the Hitlers who build the things that endure.

With this reminder of human mortality, we come around to the point where we began—to the traditional healer, who, by experimentation and esoteric lore, did his best to restore the sick to health; and we return to the bereaved kinsfolk and their fellow townsmen wailing beside the dead. Sorrow and sympathy make all men kin, and, united at the deathbed of mortal man, they give meaning to the sense of dependence that is the common and emphatic theme of African religions.

When we began at the funeral rites, we referred to an Akan mourning garb bearing a symbolic design that meant

"As long as God is not dead, I shall not die." We may end where we began by pointing to another of those designs—that of a lone star. Its meaning takes us to the core of African religions: "I, son of man, like the star, the son of the sky, depend on God, and not on myself."

In this era of nuclear power, when man is able with pomp to celebrate his scientific prowess by invading the upper regions of space, this manifest sense of dependence in traditional African religions is worth bringing again to the world's notice. If men would but heed, and particularly, if those who rule the nations, big and small, would deign to heed, a sense of accountability could be awakened that could result in our world becoming a happier place to live in. The astronauts say that the view from the upper regions of space is indescribably beautiful; what we need is an aroused sense of accountability—to make this earth of ours describably fairer.

WITHDRAWN

DATE D